POST HORN GALLOP

Post Horn Gallop

A Farce

Derek Benfield

Samuel French — London
New York — Sydney — Toronto — Hollywood

Please see page iv for further copyright information

POST HORN GALLOP

This play was first produced by the Arthur Brough Players at the Leas Pavilion, Folkestone, on 5th October, 1964, with the following cast:

ADA	*Jenny Robbins*
LORD ELROOD	*Brian Moorehead*
LADY ELROOD	*Beatrix Carter*
PATRICIA	*Frances Dunn*
MISS PARTRIDGE	*Gillian Francis*
CHESTER DREADNOUGHT	*James Fairley*
BERT	*Martin Bradley*
MAGGIE	*June Wyndham Davies*
MR. CAPONE	*Darryl Kavann*
MR. WEDGWOOD	*John Samson*
GEORGE WILLIS	*Paul Barker*

Directed by JUNE WYNDHAM DAVIES
Setting by GEORGE ETTWELL

The scene throughout is the baronial hall of Elrood Castle. The time is the present.

ACT ONE	*An Autumn morning*
ACT TWO	*Afternoon, the same day*
ACT THREE	*Evening, the same day*

No character in this play is intended to portray any specific person, alive or dead.

The running time of this play, excluding intervals, is approximately one hour and fifty-five minutes.

ACT I

The baronial hall of Elrood Castle. It is morning on a sunny Autumn day.

An imposing fireplace is in the centre of the back wall with oak panelled walls to L. and R. of it. The main entrance is through an archway U.L.C. which leads to the front door, dining-room, library, etc. Stage right is a staircase leading up to a small landing and off to the R. Below this, in the D.R. corner, is a door leading down to the cellar. There is another door U.L. which leads to the study and below which is a large mullioned window. To the R. of the fireplace, and midway between it and the staircase, is a secret door in the panelled wall which opens onstage to the R. and is only visible when it is open. Above the fireplace is a heavy portrait of a lady painted in the manner of Rubens. A bell cord is L. of the fireplace. A comfortable sofa is set at a slight angle R.C., with a table behind it, and a matching armchair L.C. with a small table on its R. on which is the telephone and a table lamp. There is a large chest in front of the window and a standard lamp in the corner U.L. Other furniture at the discretion of the producer. The furniture and dressing is tasteful and expensive and provides a warm contrast to the cold, mediaeval architecture.

ADA, *the maid, comes in with a cardboard box packed with groceries. She is crying. As she gets to C. the telephone rings. At first she is undecided what to do, then tries to answer it but almost drops the groceries. She puts the box on the sofa table and goes to the telephone. It stops ringing. She picks up the box again. The telephone rings. She puts the box down quickly and runs to the telephone. It stops ringing. She goes back as if to pick up the box but instead turns and runs back to the telephone. It starts to ring as she reaches it. She snatches up the receiver and there is a loud bang from offstage. She screams and drops the telephone.* LORD ELROOD, *a fiery war-horse of a man, comes pounding on. He carries an ancient shot-gun. He sees her at the telephone.*

ELROOD Thought as much!

ADA What, sir?

ELROOD Trying to communicate with the enemy, eh?

ADA It rang, sir.

ELROOD (*moving to her*) Rang, eh? A likely story! I never heard it ring.

ADA I expect you were too busy shooting, sir.

ELROOD Lucky for the rest of you that I was. Someone has to keep an eye on the enemy, or we'd all be overwhelmed. What did you say?

ADA I said I expect you were too busy shooting, sir.

ELROOD On the 'phone! On the 'phone!

ADA Oh—nothing, sir.

ELROOD You pick up the 'phone and say nothing? Expect me to believe that?

ADA It's true, sir.

ELROOD (*pointing the gun at her*) You'd better come clean. Why are you dressed like that?

ADA I've been to the grocer's.

ELROOD Is that how you dress when you go to the grocer's?

ADA Oh, yes.

ELROOD I don't like the look of that hat. Who are you, anyway?

ADA I'm Ada, sir. The maid.

ELROOD The maid, eh? Never seen a maid with a hat like that before. You won't last long if you go about wearing the grocer's hat.

ADA It's not the grocer's hat. It's my hat. The one I go out in.

ELROOD Don't tell me we've got a maid who goes out with the grocer.

ADA (*patiently*) To the grocer's, sir. To get the food.

ELROOD Why can't he bring the food himself?

ADA He doesn't dare.

ELROOD Why not?

ADA He says you'd shoot at him.

ELROOD I will if he wears that hat. (*Moving to below the sofa.*) Lucky I didn't see you coming across the moat. Might have mistaken you for the grocer and taken a pot shot. You know what a pot shot is, don't you?

ADA Yes, sir.

ELROOD Well, I might have taken one. (*Seeing the box of groceries.*) What's all this?

ADA The food, sir.

ELROOD (*suspiciously*) From the grocer?

ADA Yes, sir.

ELROOD Take cover!

(*He drags her down behind the armchair. After a moment they peer out, he R. of it, she L.*)

Listen! Can you hear anything?

ADA No, sir.

ELROOD Funny. You wait here. Better make sure. (*He creeps across to the sofa, listens intently, takes out a packet from the box and throws it, grenade-fashion, upstage.*) Look out!

(*They both put their heads down. A pause, then, satisfied, he straightens up.*)

All clear.

ADA (*creeping out*) What was it, sir?

ELROOD Had to be certain. Might have been a time bomb.

(*The telephone rings. They both jump.*)

ADA Shall I answer it?

ELROOD Leave it to me. (*He picks up the receiver.*) You're wasting your time. There's nobody here. (*He hangs up.*) That's the only way to deal with 'em. So this is your first day here?

ADA (*wearily*) No, sir. I've been here six months now.

ELROOD Thought I knew the face. (*Crossing to the foot of the stairs.*) Well, I must be off. Better have a word with Horatio.

ADA Horatio, sir?

ELROOD Don't tell me you've been here six months and not met Horatio? He's in charge of the drawbridge. Better have it raised now you're safely back. (*He stomps off up the stairs.*)

(ADA *sighs, picks up the box of food again as* LADY ELROOD *comes in from the study. She is wearing a housecoat and a vague air and carries a cup of coffee. She comes to C.*)

LADY E. Was that my husband?

ADA Yes, ma'am. He's gone to raise the drawbridge.

LADY E. Oh, dear. It's such a pity. Perhaps we ought to have a drawbridge built for him one day. It must be so frustrating having to pretend all the time.

ADA He doesn't seem to mind. You know, I've been here six months and I 'aven't got used to him yet. None of the tradespeople will deliver now. Every time they come near the place his lordship starts shooting at them.

LADY E. (*reasonably*) It's only because he thinks it's the postman in disguise. (*To below the armchair.*)

ADA And that makes it all right?

LADY E. Well, he always has fired at the postman. You must be more tolerant, Emily. (*She sits in the armchair and stirs her coffee.*)

ADA Ada, ma'am.

LADY E. H'm?

ADA My name's Ada.

LADY E. Is it?

ADA It's been Ada for six months, ma'am.

LADY E. *I*'ve never called you that before.

ADA (*wearily*) No, madam.

LADY E. I can't change now. You should have told me before. Now, have you got the room ready?

ADA The room?

LADY E. For my daughter and her husband.
(ADA *starts to cry softly.*)
Now, Emily—there's nothing to cry about. If you haven't done it there's still time. They won't be arriving just yet.
(ADA *cries loudly.*)
Now, pull yourself together. I'm not angry with you. I only asked if you'd done it.

ADA That's not what I'm crying about, ma'am.

LADY E. Isn't it? Oh, I am glad. Then what *are* you crying about?

ADA 'im!

LADY E. 'im?

ADA Yes—'im—'im and 'er.

LADY E. 'im and 'er? Good heavens! Who do you mean?

ADA Miss Patricia—and 'im!

LADY E. You mean Chester?

ADA Yes'm—'im! (*Cries loudly.*)

LADY E. Well, he's not as bad as all that. He's quite a nice young man, really. And anyhow even if he was horrible there's no need for you to cry. It's Patricia who married him.

ADA Yes'm—that's why I'm crying! (*She cries.*)

LADY E. Well, that's very thoughtful of you, but you needn't be upset for Patricia. She's very happy.

ADA You don't understand——

LADY E (*rising, putting her coffee cup on the armchair table*) You mean she isn't happy?

ADA No, ma'am. She is, and I'm not. It's 'im and 'er!

LADY E. Yes, I know—you said so——

ADA (*to below the sofa*) And I wanted it to be 'im and me! (*She cries again.*)

LADY E. Oh, dear. I never realised.

ADA Ever since he first set foot here I've had a passion for 'im.

LADY E. (*to her*) Oh, I am sorry.

ADA And he gave me the impression that he liked me. He led me on.

LADY E. Oh, I'm sure you're mistaken.

ADA He led me on, he did.

LADY E. I expect you misunderstood.

ADA He led me on, then he led her off.

LADY E. Off?

ADA To the altar.

LADY E. And you must accept it—and be brave. After all, we can't have you crying all over the place when they arrive. This is to be a happy occasion.
(*ADA cries loudly.*)
If you're going to cry, for heaven's sake put down the groceries. You'll make the spaghetti all soggy.

ADA Here!
(*She dumps the box into* LADY ELROOD'S *hands, sits on the sofa and continues crying. There is a loud report from offstage.* ADA *jumps.* LADY ELROOD *does not.*)
There! He's at it again!

LADY E. (*puzzled*) It's a bit late for the postman. (*She puts the box of groceries on the sofa table.*)
(LORD ELROOD *charges on with his shotgun at the ready.*)
(*casually*) Good morning, dear.

ELROOD Thinks he'll fool me by dressing up in a coat and hat, eh? Ha! ha! I'll show him! (*He runs across and out through the archway.*)

LADY E. He used to be such a quiet man in the Indian Civil.

ADA One day he's going to really hit someone, then there'll be trouble.
(*A loud report from offstage.* ELROOD *returns. He comes to* C., *on* L. *of* LADY ELROOD.)

ELROOD He ran like the devil but I think I winged him.

LADY E. Well done, dear!

ELROOD No subtlety, these Russian spies. Dressing up all the time. Do you know, he still comes in that damn uniform sometimes!

LADY E. (*as if to a child*) That's the postman, dear.

ELROOD Postman? That's what he'd like me to think. This time he was wearing a red hat and a fur coat. Looked for all the world like a woman. (*He makes for the stairs* R.) Still, I gave him a couple of blasts. That should settle him.

LADY E. Will you be down for dinner to-night, dear?

ELROOD (*going up the stairs*) No chance, I'm afraid. I'll have some bully with the men. Marcellus! Fall out the guard! (*He goes.*)

ADA (*rising*) Have you ever thought of having him seen to, ma'am?

LADY E. Seen to? (*Crossing to her coffee.*) Whatever do you mean?

ADA By one of them psychologicalists.

LADY E. Henry see a headshrinker? Oh, no, Emily! You think he's mad? Just because he imagines we've got a moat and a drawbridge and that the postman's a spy? Of course not. He's perfectly normal.
(PATRICIA *comes in from the archway, breathless, carrying a suitcase and wearing a fur coat and a red hat. She is a pretty girl in her middle twenties. She comes to* C.)

PATRICIA You know, one of these days father's really going to hurt somebody. He didn't even recognise me!

LADY E. Pat! It wasn't you? (*She puts down her coffee again.*)

PATRICIA It certainly was. I had to run like a gazelle. It's so undignified.

(LADY ELROOD *and* PATRICIA *embrace.*)

LADY E. Hullo, darling. You look marvellous!

PATRICIA Thank you, mummy.

LADY E. You didn't say what time you'd be arriving.

PATRICIA We weren't sure about trains and things. (*Looking about.*) Everything looks just the same.

LADY E. Yes, dear. I'm sorry. If I'd known what time you'd be here I'd have dressed.

PATRICIA Oh, I didn't mean that! (*To below the sofa.*) Hullo, Ada. How nice to see you again.

(ADA, *fighting her tears, goes round the* R. *end of the sofa to above it and takes up the groceries.*)

ADA I'd better get these put away. (*She creeps towards the archway.*)

(PATRICIA *looks inquiringly at* LADY ELROOD, *who shrugs and sits with her coffee in the armchair.*)

LADY E. Where's Chester? Seeing to the rest of the luggage?

PATRICIA No, mummy.

LADY E. No?

(ADA *stops at the door but does not turn, listening.*)

PATRICIA I'm afraid I lost him.

LADY E. Lost him? That was very careless of you.

PATRICIA He just disappeared on Victoria Station.

LADY E. And left you?

PATRICIA Yes.

(ADA *turns, her face brightening with hope.*)

ADA He's left you, miss?

PATRICIA In a way, yes.

ADA (*enthusiastically*) Oh, I *am* glad to see you! (*She goes out, radiant.*)

PATRICIA Whatever's the matter with her?

LADY E. She's a little overwrought. She's been to the grocer's.

PATRICIA Is that the effect he has on her?

LADY E. Oh, no. I simply meant that she was overwrought and she'd been to the grocer's. Completely disconnected.

PATRICIA I should hope so.

(*The telephone rings.*)

LADY E. (*rising*) Will you answer it, dear? It's probably the fishmonger.

PATRICIA Well, he won't want to speak to me, will he?

LADY E. No. He'll want to speak to me.

PATRICIA Well——?

LADY E. I don't want to speak to him. He's being very unreasonable and I refuse to argue with him. Tell him I'm out.

(*She breaks away to the window, D.L.*)

(PATRICIA *takes up the receiver.*)

PATRICIA I'm afraid she's out at the moment. Oh, it's you, darling! (*To* LADY E.) It's him, darling.

LADY E. Is he still at Victoria Station?

PATRICIA No, I was talking to Mummy. I said it was you. Oh, the fishmonger, I think. She was expecting him. Yes, she's just here. I don't know why she didn't answer the 'phone if she was expecting the fishmonger.

LADY E. Is he still on Victoria Station?

PATRICIA Are you still on Victoria Station? Well, that's where I last saw you. Don't you remember? (*To* LADY E.) No, he's not there any more. (*Into the telephone.*) Where are you now? Well, why don't you come on in, then? Oh, I see. I'll tell him, but for heaven's sake hurry up. (*She hangs up.*) He's in the village.

LADY E. He ought to be here.

PATRICIA He says he'll be waving a white handkerchief and to make sure that Daddy holds his fire.

LADY E. Poor boy. It must be so disconcerting having a father-in-law who greets you with a barrelful of buckshot.

(*A loud report from offstage.*)

PATRICIA He can't be here already!

LADY E. Oh, no. That'll be that nice boy from the greengrocer's. He always tries twice. (*Moving to her.*) Darling, you are happy, aren't you?

PATRICIA Yes, Mother, of course I am.

LADY E. It's just that Chester seems to be behaving so oddly.

PATRICIA Well, he was all right up until yesterday afternoon.

LADY E. What happened then?

PATRICIA He was quietly reading the evening paper when suddenly he jumped up and shouted 'They're out!' and begin to shiver all over.

LADY E. *(sitting in the armchair)* How very strange. What caused it?

PATRICIA He couldn't tell me.

LADY E. Couldn't? Or wouldn't?

PATRICIA *(taking off her coat and putting it on the end of the sofa)* Couldn't. Every time he tried he shook so violently that his teeth chattered and I couldn't understand a word. Ever since then he's been behaving very mysteriously—opening doors carefully and peering behind curtains like some sort of heavy spy. Last night he even looked under the bed. I can't imagine what's come over him.

LADY E. Too much television, that's what it is, dear.

PATRICIA Well, perhaps a few days peace and quiet here in the country will put him right.

LADY E. *(doubtfully)* Er—yes, dear.

PATRICIA You sound doubtful.

LADY E. Well, as a matter of fact—it may not be all that peaceful.

PATRICIA You mean Daddy? Oh, Chester's used to that. Once he's run the gauntlet of getting into the place everything will be all right.

LADY E. I don't mean your father.

PATRICIA Then what do you mean? It'll be peaceful apart from him, won't it?

LADY E. No. I'm—I'm afraid it won't.

PATRICIA *(to R. of LADY ELROOD)* Why not?

(LADY ELROOD rises, embarrassed, and moves away D.L.)

LADY E. Well, darling, this is a very expensive place to keep up, you know.

PATRICIA Why should that make it less peaceful?

LADY E. *(turning to face her)* Well—er—it'll be the people.

PATRICIA What people?

LADY E. The general public. We're opening the castle to the general public. Half a crown a time. *(With more enthusiasm.)* Three shillings on Saturdays.

(PATRICIA crosses to LADY ELROOD and hugs her.)

PATRICIA Oh, my poor darling!

LADY E. It's not as bad as all that. A lot of people do it, you know. It doesn't mean we're on the bread line. Well, it does—but a lot of people do it who aren't: if you know what I mean.

PATRICIA And when is all this going to start?

LADY E. On the seventeenth.

PATRICIA When's that?

LADY E. Two or three days, I think.

PATRICIA Well, what's to-day? (*She gets a newspaper from the armchair table and looks at it.*) The seventeenth!

LADY E. It can't be.

PATRICIA It is! Look! (*They meet below the armchair and peer at the newspaper.*)

LADY E. Good heavens! That means there'll be hordes of people arriving at any moment!

(ADA *comes in from the archway to* C.)

ADA Miss Partridge is here, madam.

LADY E. Tell her to go away.

ADA She says you're expecting her.

LADY E. Am I? Oh, dear!

PATRICIA I remember her. Isn't she that woman from the Archaeological Society? You know—she was studying Roman remains and wrote a book called 'Fossils I Have Known'.

LADY E. Was her name Partridge?

PATRICIA I think so.

ADA Well, shall I bring her in or throw her out?

LADY E. You'd better bring her in, I suppose, Emily.

ADA Ada!

LADY E. H'm?

ADA Ada! (*She goes.*)

LADY E. That girl gets worse.

PATRICIA (*taking off her hat and crossing to the sofa*) Well, it is time you learned her name, you know.

LADY E. (*suddenly*) A guide!

PATRICIA I beg your pardon?

LADY E. That's why she's coming.

PATRICIA Who?

LADY E. This Partridge thing. She's going to be a guide.

PATRICIA Isn't she a bit old for that?

LADY E. A guide for the visitors.

PATRICIA I thought you meant a Girl Guide. (*She sits on the* R. *end of the sofa.*)

LADY E. I thought she could explain the history of the place better than I could.

(ADA *comes in.*)

ADA Miss Partridge!

(ADA *withdraws.* MISS PARTRIDGE *enters. She is an eccentric woman in her early forties, laden with large handbag, a mallet, a magnifying glass, etc. She gazes about rapturously, coming to* C.)

MISS P. Oh, if these walls could only speak. Such atmosphere! Such history! As I enter I can feel the vibrations of the past.

LADY E. (*moving to meet her*) How are you, Miss Partridge? I do hope——

MISS P. Sh'sh! (*She crosses below* LADY ELROOD *to* D.L.) Listen! (*She listens intently.*) Did you hear that?

LADY E. (*exchanging a glance with* PATRICIA) Er—no, I'm afraid——

MISS P. Echoes of Charles the Second.

LADY E. I'm so glad. Won't you sit down?

MISS P. I wonder if you know how lucky you are, Lady Elrood, to live in such a mesh of memories! Fascinating! Fascinating!

LADY E. You remember my daughter, don't you?

MISS P. Yes. Has something happened to her?

LADY E. No. She's over there.

MISS P. (*crossing to* D.C.) Oh—this is your daughter? Of course it is. Silly of me. You look different.

LADY E. She's married.

MISS P. I thought there was something. (*She proceeds to the fireplace and peers up the chimney.*) Oo—ee! (*There is an answering echo from the chimney.*) Oo—ee! (*Again the echo.*) Amazing!

LADY E. Miss Partridge, I asked you to come and see me——

MISS P. (*moving down to* C.) I'd have had to return here one day even if you hadn't asked me. To breathe the air of antiquity! (*She breathes the air of antiquity.*)

LADY E. There was a special reason for my asking you here. I want a guide for the visitors who will be coming to look over the castle and I thought—with your expert knowledge—you'd be the ideal person.

MISS P. (*horrified*) People—coming—here?

LADY E. Yes. Sightseers.

MISS P. Heavy-footed imbeciles disturbing the relics of the past!

LADY E. I know it's a shame but——

MISS P. Inane laughter jangling with the music of medieval times!

LADY E. I thought if you were here, Miss Partridge, you could link the present with the past. And with you in charge I'm sure there would be no hooliganism. I'm sure the people would find it most instructive.

MISS P. (*weakening*) I'm flattered—flattered!

LADY E. Then you'll do it?

MISS P. I'd be delighted.

LADY E. I'm so glad.

    (*A loud report from offstage.* PATRICIA *jumps up.*)

PATRICIA Oh! I never told Daddy to hold his fire! (*Running off.*) Daddy! Daddy, don't shoot! Don't shoot! (*She goes off upstairs.*)

LADY E. You mustn't take any notice of my husband.

MISS P. (*looking around*) Is he here?

LADY E. No. He's up there. That was him shooting.

MISS P. (*to below the sofa*) Now—when do I start?

LADY E. To-day, I'm afraid. I'm sorry it's such short notice, but I got a little confused over dates.

MISS P. Ah, yes—I'm the same. I often mix up the Battle of Bannockburn 1314 with the Battle of Agincourt 1415—

LADY E. (*to L. of fireplace*) If you'd care to live here for a while so you're on the spot you can have the west turret room. I'll have your things brought for you from the village.

MISS P. Very thoughtful of you, Lady Elrood.

LADY E. (*ringing the bell*) I'll get the maid to show you to your room. (*She takes an armband with the word 'GUIDE' on it from the mantelpiece and comes to L. of* MISS PARTRIDGE.) Now, I thought perhaps you could wear this then everyone will know who you are.

MISS P. Ah, capital! Very apt indeed. (*She tries to put it on her head.*) A little small, I fear——

LADY E. I think it goes on the arm, Miss Partridge.

MISS P. H'm? Oh, yes! Yes, of course! (*She puts it on her arm.*) (ADA *comes in to* L. *of* LADY ELROOD.)

ADA You rang, ma'am?

LADY E. Oh, yes. Now, Edna——

ADA Ada!

LADY E. Yes. This is Miss Partridge.

MISS P. (*beaming*) Guide!

ADA Eh?

MISS P. Guide!

ADA (*to* LADY ELROOD) I thought you said her name was Partridge.

LADY E. Yes, it is.

MISS P. Guide!

ADA Well, which is it?

LADY E. Her name is Partridge.

ADA Well, you'd better tell her that! (MISS PARTRIDGE *takes out a magnifying glass and peers at the wall* D.R.)

LADY E. She'll be staying in the little room in the West Turret. Will you show her there, please?

ADA Shall I take your suitcase?

LADY E. No.

ADA You mean she'll carry it herself?

LADY E. I mean there's no suitcase.

ADA (*suspiciously*) I see. This way, Miss Guide. (*Makes for the archway.*)

LADY E. (*loudly*) Partridge!

MISS P. (*turning*) Yes?

LADY E. I was talking to the maid.

ADA My name's not Partridge.

LADY E. No, but hers is.

ADA This way, Miss Partridge. (*She goes out, leading the way.*) (MISS PARTRIDGE *crosses to the archway, hesitates.*)

MISS P. In the West Turret I shall be closer to Cromwell than I've ever been in my life! (*She goes.*) (PATRICIA *returns, agitated.*)

PATRICIA I was too late. Daddy says he may have winged him.
LADY E. Who? (*She meets* PATRICIA *D.R.*)
PATRICIA Chester.
LADY E. Oh, no!
PATRICIA Isn't it awful?
LADY E. It certainly is. I haven't even dressed yet. (*She starts up the stairs.*)
PATRICIA Mummy—he may be dying!
LADY E. Well, keep him alive till I get back. (*She goes.*)
PATRICIA Bandages! (*She goes off through the study door.*)
          (*The stage is empty for a moment. Then* CHESTER DREAD-NOUGHT'S *head appears cautiously from the archway, and seeing all is clear he comes in. He is a good-looking young man of about 30 and is a trifle breathless. He wears a casual suit and carries a suitcase and a raincoat. He peers behind the sofa, backs slowly into the armchair table and almost knocks the lamp off it. He opens the lid of the chest cautiously and is looking inside it as* PATRICIA *returns. She comes down to his R.*)
          Darling!
          (CHESTER *jumps with fright, slamming the lid of the chest.*)
CHESTER Oh, it's you.
PATRICIA What on earth are you doing?
CHESTER Now? Nothing.
PATRICIA When I came in.
CHESTER Oh, then! Yes—I was looking.
PATRICIA Looking?
CHESTER In the chest. I was looking in the chest.
PATRICIA What for?
CHESTER I didn't find it. I was looking in the chest and I didn't.
PATRICIA Did you expect there to be something in the chest?
CHESTER I should hope so. Not much point in having a chest if there's nothing in it. It might have been full. Old riding boots, socks—things like that.
PATRICIA Is that why you were looking?
CHESTER Yes. I thought I might have a canter before lunch.
PATRICIA Chester, what is the matter with you?
CHESTER Nothing, darling.

PATRICIA (*leading him to the sofa*) Come and sit down here and let me see to it.

CHESTER Righto. (*They sit on the sofa.*) See to what?

PATRICIA I'll have to stop it.

CHESTER I didn't know you'd started.

PATRICIA (*impatiently*) Stop the bleeding!

CHESTER Now, now! There's no need for that!

PATRICIA (*showing him the bandage*) What do you think these are for?

CHESTER The horse's hocks?

PATRICIA What horse?

CHESTER The one I'm going to have a canter on before lunch.

PATRICIA They're for you.

CHESTER (*gratefully*) Oh, you shouldn't have bothered.

PATRICIA Where is it?

CHESTER Ah, yes—where is it?

PATRICIA Where is the bleeding? The wound!

CHESTER Oh—the wound. Ah, yes, I haven't got that.

PATRICIA You haven't?

CHESTER No. Nothing like it.

PATRICIA Daddy missed then?

CHESTER Oh, coming in? Yes, he did. But only just.

PATRICIA So you're not dying?

CHESTER Not yet.

PATRICIA I'll put these away then.

CHESTER I should keep them handy. Their turn may come. (PATRICIA *puts the bandages on the table behind the sofa and snuggles up to him.*)

PATRICIA Oh, darling!

CHESTER Be careful. Your mother may come in.

PATRICIA What does it matter? We're married.

CHESTER So we are. I keep forgetting.

PATRICIA You're not very demonstrative.

CHESTER Well, I haven't unpacked yet.

PATRICIA Ada'll do that.

CHESTER Ada?

PATRICIA The maid.

CHESTER Good lord! Is she still here?

PATRICIA You don't mind, do you, darling?

CHESTER What—the maid still being here?

PATRICIA Coming here for a few days.

CHESTER It'll be nice to have some peace and quiet. (*He rises and moves L. nervously.*)

PATRICIA (*a little hurt*) What do you mean by that?

CHESTER In the country—no 'buses—bicycles—jangling and hooting—hooting and jangling—you know. (*He looks behind the curtains.*)

PATRICIA (*rising*) Darling, you are all right, aren't you? I don't know what's come over you. Are you ill or not?

CHESTER (*to below the armchair*) Oh, not. Definitely not.

PATRICIA You've been acting so mysteriously. All this looking behind curtains and in chests and things—anyone would think someone was after you.

CHESTER Would they? (*He laughs but lets it die.*)

PATRICIA (*to him*) You can tell me, darling. Is there something wrong?

CHESTER Yes. Very. Something very.

PATRICIA Well, what is it?

CHESTER Those two men.

PATRICIA What two men?

CHESTER Don't you remember before we were married there were two men——

PATRICIA (*smiling*) You're not jealous, are you?

CHESTER Oh, not that kind of man. These two men went to prison.

PATRICIA What about it?

CHESTER Because of me, don't you remember?

PATRICIA Oh, those two men! But you only did your duty. They'd robbed a bank and you gave evidence against them.

CHESTER Exactly. (*He crosses below her to D.C.*) Well, they're out.

PATRICIA Of the bank?

CHESTER Of prison. Yesterday. I saw it in the paper.

PATRICIA (*to him*) What of it?

CHESTER I'm worried.

PATRICIA What about?

CHESTER They may want something.

PATRICIA What?

CHESTER My blood.

PATRICIA Don't be silly, darling.

CHESTER I remember the last words old Capone—that was his name, Capone—the last words he said to me when they took him away—'I'll get you when I come out," he said.

PATRICIA He wasn't serious.

CHESTER He didn't smile.

PATRICIA Darling, they'd never come after you. Anyhow, they'd never get in here. Father would take a pot shot at them if they came anywhere near.

CHESTER (smiles) Yes—yes, of course! (Sobering.) He might miss. Still, I suppose you're right—they couldn't really get in here, could they?
(PATRICIA has gone silent. He looks at her.)
What's the matter, darling?

PATRICIA Oh, nothing—nothing at all. (Breaks slightly to L.)

CHESTER (following her) You've gone all peculiar. What is it? You've thought of something. What is it?

PATRICIA (fearfully) It's just that—from to-day Mummy has opened up the castle to the general public!

CHESTER What?

PATRICIA At two-and-six a time.

CHESTER Two-and-six?

PATRICIA Three shillings on Saturdays.

CHESTER So these men can pay two-and-six and walk straight in here?

PATRICIA Yes!

CHESTER Oh, my God! (He crosses below her to D.L.)

PATRICIA Where are you going?

CHESTER To get in the chest. (He opens it.)

PATRICIA That's the first place they'd look.

CHESTER Is it?

PATRICIA It was the first place you looked.

CHESTER Ah, yes—but I was looking for riding boots.

PATRICIA Besides, you'd suffocate.

CHESTER That's all right—then they can't shoot me. (He starts to get into the chest.)

PATRICIA Chester, get out of there!

CHESTER It's all your father's fault. If he'd been a better shot I'd be dead by now. What are we going to do?

PATRICIA We'll think of something.

CHESTER It'll have to be quick. They're probably outside now fumbling for their small change.

PATRICIA I tell you what—I'll go and ask Mummy not to open the gates to the public until after we've gone home. (*Crosses to D.R.*)

CHESTER It may be too late.

PATRICIA I won't be long. You stay here—and Chester——

CHESTER Yes, darling?

PATRICIA Be brave! (*She goes off up the stairs.*)

CHESTER It's all right for you. All you have to do is cash the policies. Be brave, she says. Ha! She's right, of course. I've nothing to fear. What can they do to me? Nothing at all. Only kill me.

(*He sits on the sofa and gets out his cigarettes. ADA peers around the archway, sees him and tiptoes down to behind the sofa. He senses an approach and looks slowly to his R. As he does so, she moves slightly to his L. He turns slowly to his L., while she moves slightly to his R. He sees nothing, shrugs it off and relaxes.*)

ADA Oh, sir!

(*He jumps a mile and drops the cigarettes onto the floor.*) I'll pick them up for you. (*She kneels at his feet and picks them up, gazing at him adoringly.*)

CHESTER Why did you have to do that? Creeping up behind me like a ghost in a pantomime.

ADA I wanted to give you a warm welcome, sir.

CHESTER Well, you did. Very warm. Too warm.

ADA (*handing him the cigarettes*) There you are, sir.

CHESTER Thank you. Just look at me—you've made me shake all over.

ADA (*sitting beside him*) That's a good sign, sir.

CHESTER Oh, is it? Thank you very much. Is this yours? (*He gives her back her hand which is on his knee.*)

ADA I heard about you, sir.

CHESTER Did you? Good heavens!

ADA (*knowingly*) On Victoria Station.

CHESTER Yes, I was. This morning.

ADA I heard what you did, sir. (*She giggles and nudges him.*)

CHESTER I didn't do that, did I?

ADA So I knew there was still hope.

CHESTER Hope?

ADA For me.

CHESTER Why? Do you want to go to Victoria Station? It's very ordinary, I assure you. Lines and platforms and things. And little trains going——

ADA I knew you'd come back.

CHESTER Ah! Only for the weekend.

ADA A weekend can be a lifetime! (*She moves nearer.*)

CHESTER Now, look here—Ada—— (*He eludes her and perches on the* L. *arm of the sofa.*)

ADA You remembered my name!

CHESTER Well, yes—I——

ADA Nobody ever remembers my name. It must be a portent.

CHESTER A what?

ADA A portent.

CHESTER Oh, I wouldn't say it was that.

ADA (*smiling*) I was sorry to hear about your marriage, sir.

CHESTER It's not as bad as all that.

ADA You mean you aren't sorry?

CHESTER Not at all. I'm rather glad.

ADA Then you did come back for me!

CHESTER No. I came back for the weekend.

ADA For *me* for the weekend!

CHESTER What are you talking about?

ADA (*moving closer*) You're in love with me, sir!
(*A loud report from offstage. He falls into her arms. She enjoys it.* CHESTER *realises what he is doing and extricates himself.*)
Do it again, sir!

CHESTER Now, now! That was an accident.

ADA Call it what you like, sir, but do it again.

CHESTER I don't know what's come over you, Ada. Not a crocus in sight and you're going raving mad.
(LORD ELROOD *comes quickly down the stairs with his shotgun.*)

ELROOD Ah, you're here at last! About time, too.

CHESTER We were held up, sir.

ELROOD Didn't you get my note?

CHESTER Note?

ELROOD The memo! The memo!

CHESTER Afraid not. Afraid not.

ELROOD Reinforcements, blast it! Reinforcements!

CHESTER Oh, no, never.

ELROOD But you're here, man! Must have got it if you're here. Blasted incompetence! Young subalterns—still wet behind the ears.

CHESTER Wet, sir? I mean—what, sir?

ELROOD If you didn't get my memo why the hell are you here?

CHESTER We've come for the weekend.

ADA For *me* for the weekend!

CHESTER Go away!

ELROOD For the weekend? What do you think this is—damned Territorials or something? Weekend, indeed. You did come from reserve, didn't you?

CHESTER No, we came from Victoria.

ELROOD Reserve battalion!

CHESTER Look, Father——

ELROOD Father? Don't be impertinent! Now you're here you may as well make yourself useful. You'll relieve Marcellus.

CHESTER Marcellus?

ELROOD He's the Captain of the Guard. Time he had a break, He's been a bit jumpy lately.

CHESTER I'm not surprised.

ELROOD What did you say?

CHESTER I said it must be his size. Big, tall fellow like that—always the first to go.

ELROOD (*to* ADA) You—whatsyourname——

ADA (*rising*) Ada, sir.

ELROOD Oh, you're Ada? Now, do you know where he'll be sleeping?

ADA (*smiling hopefully*) I'm not certain yet, sir.

ELROOD I told you to have everything in apple pie order before he arrived. (*To* CHESTER.) Don't worry—she'll soon see to your quarters.

CHESTER Look—er—sir—it's me——

ELROOD   Of course it's you, damn it!

CHESTER Your son-in-law.

ELROOD   Son in what?

CHESTER It's Chester!

ELROOD   (*crossing to the stairs*) No Christian names here! I'm running an Army, not a holiday camp. Get unpacked and report to me in fifteen minutes.

   (ELROOD *marches off.* CHESTER *smiles weakly at* ADA.)

CHESTER That's my father-in-law.

   ADA   (*moving to him*) That was your father-in-law, you mean. Not for much longer.

CHESTER Really? He looked pretty fit to me.

   ADA   You'll be getting rid of 'im, though, won't you?

CHESTER What do you mean?

   ADA   You'll be getting rid of 'im along with 'er.

CHESTER Along with 'er? Will I?

   ADA   Get rid of 'er first and 'im after.

CHESTER What are you talking about?

   (PATRICIA *and* LADY ELROOD *come downstairs.* LADY ELROOD *is now dressed.* CHESTER *crosses to meet her below the sofa.* PATRICIA *is behind her mother.*)

LADY E. Chester, dear boy, how nice to see you.

CHESTER Hullo, mother-in-law.

LADY E. You can't call me that.

CHESTER Why not? You are, aren't you?

   ADA   (*quietly*) Not for much longer she ain't.

CHESTER Be quiet.

   ADA   She'll go, too.

LADY E. What did you say?

   ADA   (*quietly*) Along with 'im and along with 'er.

CHESTER Will you be quiet?

LADY E. That will be all.

   ADA   Yes, Ma'am. (*She starts for the archway.*)

PATRICIA (*moving to* CHESTER) Darling, you're looking all jumpy. You must calm down. (*She embraces him.*)

   ADA   (*returning to* L. *of* CHESTER) Here! What's this?

LADY E. I told you that would be all.

   ADA   What's going on? I thought you were getting rid of 'er?

CHESTER Certainly not. She's my wife.

ADA	I thought that was all over.
CHESTER	Over? Not nearly.
ADA	Then you're not free?
CHESTER	Definitely not.
ADA	(*bursting into tears*) O-o-o-oh! (*She makes for the archway and goes off, crying loudly.*)
PATRICIA	Whatever's the matter with her?
LADY E.	I think she thought you were unhappy.
PATRICIA	And now she's crying because we aren't?
LADY E.	(*vaguely*) Yes. I think that's what she said. Take no notice of her. These highly-strung village girls are all the same.
CHESTER	Darling, did you speak to your mother?
PATRICIA	Oh, yes. She says you've nothing to worry about.
CHESTER	(*crossing to* LADY ELROOD) Is that what you said?
LADY E.	Yes. You've nothing to worry about.
CHESTER	That is a relief! So you won't let anyone in to look around until after we've gone?
PATRICIA	Well—er—not exactly, darling.
CHESTER	What do you mean not exactly?
PATRICIA	(*reasonably*) Well, Mummy does need the money.
CHESTER	Does it have to be blood money?
PATRICIA	Mummy says if anyone acts at all suspiciously she'll send for the Police.
CHESTER	That's very comforting. You mean, if she sees someone standing over my limp body with a smoking gun in his hand?
PATRICIA	There's no need to talk like that. (*She moves away to D.L.C.*)
CHESTER	What do you mean? How do you expect me to talk? (*To* LADY ELROOD.) You may as well put up a notice outside—'Come and shoot at Chester Dreadnought, two-and-six a time!'
	(MISS PARTRIDGE *comes in through the archway. She sees them and comes to* L. *of* CHESTER.)
MISS P.	Ah! you must be the first arrivals! Welcome to Elrood Castle.
LADY E.	(*crossing below* CHESTER *to* MISS PARTRIDGE) Miss Partridge——

MISS P. Now, perhaps a short historical résumé before we begin to——

LADY E. Miss Partridge——

MISS P. I am sure you'll be astonished at the relics you are about to see——

LADY E. Miss Partridge—it's me—Lady Elrood!

MISS P. (*peering at her*) H'm?

LADY E. I live here!

(MISS PARTRIDGE, *puzzled, turns to* PATRICIA.)

PATRICIA We all live here!

MISS P. Oh. I'm so sorry. Then you don't want to look around?

PATRICIA No, thank you.

MISS P. Then I must go to where I shall be of more use. (*She crosses to D.R.C., turns on R. of* CHESTER.) Guide!

CHESTER I beg your pardon?

MISS P. (*pointing to her armband*) Guide!

CHESTER Oh—congratulations!

(MISS PARTRIDGE *wanders off* D.R. CHESTER *crosses to C., making for the archway.*)

PATRICIA Where are you going?

CHESTER You don't expect me to stand about here waiting to be killed, do you?

PATRICIA (*breaking to the chest, wearily*) Darling, don't exaggerate. Those two men would never dare come in here after you—even if they wanted to. Which I very much doubt.

(*A loud report from offstage.*)

ELROOD (*off*) Where the devil are the reinforcements?

CHESTER I'll have to go. He's after me, too.

PATRICIA Daddy?

CHESTER Yes. He thinks I'm from reserve. I'll have to go and hide. (*He moves to the archway.*)

PATRICIA What shall I say to him?

CHESTER Tell him I'm looking at my quarters. (*He goes.*)

(LORD ELROOD *pounds on. He looks over the banisters.*)

ELROOD Any sign of reserve battalion?

LADY E. (*sweetly*) Not yet, I'm afraid, darling. As soon as they come we'll send them to you.

ELROOD Malingerers! Just when we need them. The enemy are

moving in. We've already spotted three or four of their advance party outside. (*He marches off.*)

LADY E. (*delighted*) That'll be the first of the sightseers. How lovely! What's four two-and-sixes?

PATRICIA Ten shillings.

LADY E. Oh. Oh, well, it's a start. Come along, Pat.

PATRICIA (*following her*) Where are we going?

LADY E. Well, we've got to make sure they've paid their money. (*They go out through the archway.*

From the study door two forlorn figures appear. A dowdy, middle-aged Cockney couple; she small and round, he thin and lugubrious. They are MAGGIE *and* BERT. *They wander to C., looking about.*)

BERT 'Alf-a-crown for this? You must be mad.

MAGGIE Don't be so ignorant. Try to broaden your outlook, for 'eaven's sake, Bert. (*She moves below the sofa to D.R.*)

BERT Anyone would think you was one of the upper classes, the way you go on.

MAGGIE You're a snob—that's what you are.

BERT Me?

MAGGIE 'Ave a look at the other side of the coin. See 'ow the other 'alf lives. (*To R. of the fireplace.*) 'Ere—look at that picture! I bet that's worth a fortune. Rubens I shouldn't be surprised.

BERT Rubens? Who's she? (*Up to L. of the fireplace.*) Indecent, that's what I call it. Look at her chest!

MAGGIE That's art, that's what that is.

BERT Art? Looks more like them Folies Bergeries. (*He moves to L. of the armchair.*) You needn't bother getting ideas. We're not 'aving anything like that in our 'ouse.

MAGGIE I wish you'd try to improve.

BERT Decadent, that's what they are. Decadent. (*He pronounces it 'decaydent'.*)

MAGGIE (*crossing to below the armchair*) You know, there's something pitiful about you, Bert. You've got no imagination. These days there's not all that difference between people like them and people like us.

BERT You try charging 'alf-a-crown to look round our 'ouse in Poplar.

MAGGIE You're suburban, you are. Suburban and middle class.

BERT I'd rather be suburban than decadent.

(MISS PARTRIDGE *comes on* D.R. *She moves briskly to* MAGGIE.)

MISS P. Ah! I've been looking for you everywhere.

BERT Oh, yes?

MISS P. (*playfully*) You slipped past. I never noticed you. You should have given me a nudge.

BERT Oh, yes?

MISS P. Didn't you see it?

BERT What?

MISS P. (*pointing to her armband*) Guide! Guide!

BERT Oh, yes?

MISS P. You'll be fascinated by the extraordinary things you'll see here.

(BERT *and* MAGGIE *exchange a look.*)

Listen to this! (*She goes to the fireplace and calls up the chimney.*) Oo-ee! (*An answering echo.*) Oo-ee! (*Again the echo.*) I bet you've never seen an echoing chimney before. (*Coming to them.*) I say, I almost forgot.

BERT Oh, yes?

MISS P. Half-a-crown.

BERT Eh?

MISS P. Half-a-crown each.

BERT But, look 'ere, we already——

MAGGIE Bert!

(*Reluctantly he fishes in his pocket and gives five shillings to* MISS PARTRIDGE. *From her bag she produces a ticket machine like those used on buses and rolls off two tickets.*)

MISS P. There we are.

(*She busies herself putting away the ticket machine, and does not see* CHESTER *who comes running in from the hall.* MAGGIE *and* BERT *watch him as he passes them, laughs self-consciously and runs off* D.R.)

(*Straightening up.*) Charles the Second!

BERT (*looking after* CHESTER) Was it?

MISS P. I can feel his presence, can't you?

BERT Not any more.

MISS P. He's been here, you know.

BERT He's gone now, though.

MISS P. Ah! you noticed?

BERT Couldn't 'elp it.

MISS P. They say he sometimes appears from up there and goes out through that wall.

BERT Well, this time he came through there and went out up there. Look out! 'Ere he comes again!

(CHESTER *returns, breathless. He races across to* MAGGIE *and* BERT.)

CHESTER (*nervously*) They're here! I saw them! They're here in the building! (*He runs off to the study.*)

BERT Didn't look much like Charles the Second to me.

MAGGIE Oh, for 'eaven's sake—use your imagination!

BERT For five bob each I expect the real thing.

MISS P. Oh, that wasn't Charles the Second.

BERT Oh, no?

(MAGGIE *and* BERT *exchange a look.*)

MISS P. The face did seem familiar, though. (*She wanders up to the fireplace and busies herself tapping walls and listening, etc.*)

(LADY ELROOD *comes in from the hall and moves down to C.*)

LADY E. Good afternoon!

BERT (*quietly*) 'Ere's another!

LADY E. I'm afraid we're not very well organised yet. I should have met you at the door. I'm Lady Elrood.

BERT Oh, yes?

MAGGIE (*putting on a posh voice and moving to* L. *of* LADY ELROOD) How do you do, milady?

LADY E. Oh—er—how do you do?

(*Business of shaking hands.* MAGGIE *tries to curtsy but falls on the floor.* BERT *suffers.* LADY ELROOD *helps* MAGGIE *up and moves to* R. *of* BERT.)

LADY E. You've met Miss Partridge?

BERT Who?

LADY E. Partridge!

MISS P. (*turning*) That's my name.

LADY E. I can safely leave you in her hands.

BERT   Oh, yes?

LADY E.   But I—I'm afraid it does cost two-and-six each.

BERT   But we've already——!

MAGGIE   Bert!
(*Reluctantly he fishes out another five shillings and gives it to* LADY ELROOD.)

LADY E.   Thank you so much. (*She goes out through the archway.*)

MAGGIE   'Ave you got no manners?

BERT   If I stay 'ere much longer I'll 'ave no money either!

MAGGIE   And you could 'ave taken your cap off.

BERT   I'll need to take it off and pass it around when I get out of 'ere. And 'ow about you? (*Imitating her.*) How do you do, milady!

MAGGIE   A few manners wouldn't come amiss from you. (*She moves away* C.)

BERT   You call that manners? Shake 'er 'and and fall on your arse?

MAGGIE   Bert!

BERT   Well, it makes me sick.

MISS P.   (*suddenly, moving down* R. *of the sofa*) I think he married someone!

BERT   Who—Charles the Second?

MISS P.   No. The young man who went through just now.

BERT   Perhaps he's trying to get away from 'er.

MAGGIE   Oh, very funny.

MISS P.   Now—follow me! (MAGGIE *jerks her head at* BERT *and they cross to* MISS PARTRIDGE.) But tread quietly. We don't want to disturb them, do we?

BERT   Who?

MISS P.   The ghosts of the past! (*She goes out D.R.*)
(MAGGIE *and* BERT *exchange a look and follow her off. From the archway come* MR. CAPONE *and* MR. WEDGWOOD. CAPONE *is tall, dark and speaks with a slight German accent.* WEDGWOOD *is shorter, plump and does not speak at all.* CAPONE *wears a dark blue suit, a raincoat and hat.* WEDGWOOD *wears a check tweed suit.*)

CAPONE   Easier than we thought, huh? Pay the money and walk straight in.
(WEDGWOOD *nods.*)

This is going to be a pleasure.

(WEDGWOOD *draws* CAPONE'*s attention to the portrait on the wall. They look at it for a moment.*)

H'm. That is the one. Not bad, h'm?

(WEDGWOOD *shrugs.*)

Worth a lot of money.

(WEDGWOOD *nods enthusiastically.*)

More perhaps than they realise. Perhaps she would care to accompany us when we leave, huh?

(WEDGWOOD *nods.*)

It will be arranged. But first we must find Mr. Dreadnought—yes?

(WEDGWOOD *nods heartily.*)

And when we find him?

(WEDGWOOD, *with accompanying noises, slowly mimes cutting* CHESTER *from throat to stomach, pulling rib cage apart and extracting his heart.*)

Exactly!

(WEDGWOOD *hears a noise, warns* CAPONE. *They take cover behind the sofa.*

CHESTER *comes on, breathless. He looks about, in the chest, etc., but does not see* CAPONE *and* WEDGWOOD. *He sits on the sofa and mops his brow with his handkerchief, exhausted.* CAPONE *and* WEDGWOOD *emerge behind* CHESTER. CHESTER *mops the back of his neck.* CAPONE *gently takes the handkerchief and mops* CHESTER'*s brow.* CHESTER *smiles, closes his eyes, leaning back.*)

CHESTER   Oh, thank you, darling. That's lovely. It's nice to relax. I'm so tired . . . (*He yawns.*) I think I'm safe for the moment. No sign of them. Come and sit down, darling. (*He pats the sofa beside him.*)

(CAPONE *and* WEDGWOOD *look at each other, then move down each side of the sofa and sit either side of him.*) H'm. That's better. Hand, please.

(*He holds out his right hand.* CAPONE *takes it.* CHESTER *yawns, extends his left hand and drops it onto* WEDGWOOD'*s right hand. For a moment he is absolutely still, his eyes closed. Then he slowly brings both hands up in front of him. He opens his eyes and sees the hands he is holding, turns his head slowly and sees* CAPONE. *He reacts, leaps up and runs out through the archway.* CAPONE *and* WEDGWOOD *race after him.*

BERT, MAGGIE *and* MISS PARTRIDGE *come in from* D.R. MAGGIE *and* BERT *to* C. MISS PARTRIDGE *remains* D.R.)

BERT Seven-and-a-tanner each for that? It's daylight robbery!

MAGGIE Do be quiet, Bert. Steep yourself in the past like the lady said.

MISS P. And this is the—(*consulting a notebook*)—the lounge hall.

MAGGIE Nice. Oh, very nice. It is a little like the first room we saw, isn't it?

BERT Oh, for 'eaven's sake, it is the same room! Fifteen bob and already we're back where we started.
(CHESTER *runs in from the archway, passes them and goes off* D.R.)
And there goes Charles the Second again!
(CAPONE *and* WEDGWOOD *come racing in. They stop near* BERT *and* MAGGIE.)

CAPONE I say—when you came in here, did you——?

BERT Oh, not again! (*Producing a pound note.*) Here—take a quid, mate—I'll buy the bloody place!

CURTAIN

ACT II

The same afternoon.
As the curtain rises ADA *comes in. She is wearing her coat and hat and carries a very small suitcase. She comes to C. As she does so a concealed panel door R. of the fireplace creaks open and a man's back begins to emerge. She screams. The man turns. It is* CHESTER.

CHESTER   S'sh! It's only me!

ADA   Oh, sir! You didn't half give me a shock.

CHESTER   Yes—and you didn't half give me one.

ADA   What were you doing in the wall, anyway?

CHESTER   In the wall? You make me sound like a death watch beetle.

ADA   And that's about what you are, too.

CHESTER   (*moving to her*) Now, Ada! Why are you all dressed up?

ADA   I'm going off.

CHESTER   Dressed up and going off?

ADA   Yes.

CHESTER   You can't leave now.

ADA   I'm a free woman.

CHESTER   But if you leave now they'll be maidless. You don't want to leave them maidless, do you?

ADA   I don't care how I leave them. I'm going off.

CHESTER   Don't keep saying you're going off. You sound like a piece of Camembert. What'll they do without you?

ADA   They'll have to do for themselves. I've done for them long enough. Now I'm packed up and going off.

CHESTER   (*looking at her suitcase*) Is that your packing?

ADA   Yes.

CHESTER   What a very little packing. Haven't you got a bigger packing?

ADA   That's the packing I came with and that's the packing I'm leaving with.

CHESTER Have you got everything in there?

ADA I shan't need much. Not where I'm going to live.

CHESTER Where's that?

ADA In a monastery.

CHESTER Are you sure?

ADA 'Course I'm sure. I won't need many clothes there.

CHESTER No, I should think you won't! Look, I think you mean
a convent.

ADA You mean what you mean, and I'll mean what I mean!

CHESTER A monastery's for men. A convent for women.

ADA Oh. (*Moving to below the armchair.*) Oh, well, I suppose
it'll have to be a convent, then.

CHESTER But *why* are you going?

ADA (*starting to cry*) Do you have to ask? Don't you know?
(*She puts down the case near the armchair.*)

CHESTER Eh?

ADA It's you! It's you what did for me.

CHESTER I don't remember that.

ADA You did for me this morning.

CHESTER What? Before lunch?

ADA When you went off with 'er.

CHESTER Which 'er?

ADA Miss Patricia!

CHESTER Oh, that 'er. Well, she is my wife, you know.

ADA I thought you were going to get rid of 'er and take me.

CHESTER I'm sure I never said that.

ADA (*crossing to him*) You did me wrong. So now I'm packed
up, dressed up and going off.

CHESTER (*joining in*)—and going off! Yes, I know. Have you
told them?

ADA They'll find out.

CHESTER You mean you haven't given notice?

ADA They'll notice soon enough.

CHESTER That's a bit hard, isn't it? After all, they've been very
good to you, and now all of a sudden you start packing
up and going off and leaving them maidless. How would
you like to be left maidless without any warning?

ADA Well, I—I can't help it—I've got to go.

CHESTER You could tell them, and then go. Think how Lady

Elrood will appreciate it if you go up to her nicely and say, 'I'm awfully sorry, Lady Elrood, but I'm going off.' She might even give you an extra week's money.

ADA I haven't had last week's yet.

CHESTER Well, there you are—you can't leave without last week's money.

ADA (breaking below the armchair) Oh, dear, I don't know what to think now. You've got me all undecided.
(A noise off—CAPONE approaching.)

CHESTER Well, think it over, Ada. I've got to be off. (He moves up to the panel door.)

ADA (following) Where are you going?

CHESTER Back into the woodwork. Here, look—you can help me.

ADA I don't see why I should. Not after you doing for me like you did.

CHESTER Look, let bygones be bygones, shall we? I need your help.

ADA Oh, all right. But I was going off——

CHESTER Look, there are two men coming—one tall and dark, the other short and fat—and I don't want to meet them, you see. Now, when they've gone you tap on this door, will you? One tap for danger, two taps for all clear. Okay?

ADA One for danger, two for all clear. All right—but I don't see——

CHESTER Look out—here they come!
(He closes the panel door. ADA goes to L. of the sofa and starts to arrange the cushions, etc. CAPONE and WEDG-WOOD come in from the archway to C. and watch her. She is self-conscious.)

CAPONE You look very busy.

ADA Yes, sir. I am. Very busy. (She crosses to the armchair and tidies there.)

CAPONE You work here?

ADA I'm the maid.

CAPONE Do you always do the housework in your coat and hat?

ADA It's such a cold morning, sir.

CAPONE Who were you talking to?

ADA Talking to?

CAPONE   Before we came in. We heard you talking to someone.

ADA   It was me, sir. I was talking to myself. I often talk to myself.

CAPONE   I am looking for a man.

ADA   (*ruefully*) You're not the only one.

CAPONE   Perhaps you have seen him?

ADA   So many people here to-day—the place being open to the public and all that.

CAPONE   Fair, slim, blue eyes, broad shoulders, about five feet ten. Have you seen such a man?

ADA   I wish I had. He sounds lovely!

CAPONE   It is rather important.

ADA   I haven't seen anyone like that.

CAPONE   Well, keep your eyes peeled.

(MISS PARTRIDGE *comes in from the archway to between* CAPONE *and* WEDGWOOD.)

MISS P.   Ah, capital! More visitors. (*Moving to them.*) Welcome to Elrood Castle.

CAPONE   Thank you. You are who?

MISS P.   I beg your pardon?

CAPONE   You—are—who?

MISS P.   Oh, foreign tourists. How splendid. I am guide. Guide to castle. See! (*She points to her armband.*) Isn't it remarkable?

CAPONE   Remarkable?

MISS P.   The atmosphere! Try it. Go on—breathe it in! Come on—altogether—breathe!

(*They all breathe in together*)

There! Did you get a whiff of the sixteenth century? Now—(*Pushes* CAPONE *out of the way and makes for the wall U.R.C.*)—let's start over here. You'll find the old woodwork fascinating, I'm sure. Listen to this! (*She taps twice on the woodwork near the panel door with her hammer.*)

(*In panic* ADA *races across, pushing* CAPONE *and* WEDGWOOD *aside, and bangs once on the wall L. of the panel door.* CAPONE *and* WEDGWOOD *are a little astonished.*)

You hear that? Now—over here!

(CAPONE *and* WEDGWOOD *go to a position so that they are* R. *of the panel door facing* R. *where* MISS PARTRIDGE *is standing.* ADA *is* L. *of the panel door.* MISS PARTRIDGE *taps twice. The panel door starts to open.* ADA *bangs once. The panel door shuts. Repeat this, the panel door shutting this time with a bang.* CAPONE *and* WEDGWOOD *turn to look at* ADA.)

CAPONE What was that?

ADA What, sir?

CAPONE A bang. Like a door closing.

ADA Oh, no, sir. It was me.

CAPONE You?

ADA I—I was dancing, sir—you know. (*She dances a Spanish dance, feet stamping, etc.*)

(CAPONE, *still suspicious, turns to face* MISS PARTRIDGE *again.*)

MISS P. Now listen to this! (*She taps twice.*)

(*The panel door opens,* CHESTER's *head appears.* ADA *pushes him back in, the door slams.* CAPONE *and* WEDG-WOOD *turn.* ADA *starts dancing again, this time taking up a rose from a vase on the mantelpiece and putting it between her teeth. As they watch her she slows down to a halt, self-conscious. She is now below the fireplace.*)

CAPONE Do you always dance when you are doing the house-work?

ADA It's the only way I can keep warm, sir.

(MISS PARTRIDGE *comes between* CAPONE *and* WEDGWOOD *and takes their arms enthusiastically.*)

MISS P. Come along! We'll begin through here.

(*She leads* CAPONE *and* WEDGWOOD *towards the cellar door.*)

CAPONE Please—you go. We will follow.

MISS P. No, no, no! You've paid your money. We'll begin with the cellar—this way! (*She pushes them out through the door and turns back to* ADA.) Well done, dear! Didn't know you were terpsichorean.

ADA I'm not. I'm Church of England.

(MISS PARTRIDGE *goes.* ADA *crosses to the wall and taps*

twice. CHESTER *comes out, closing the panel door be-*
hind him.)

CHESTER What are you playing at? Can't you make up your
mind?

ADA Miss Partridge took them into the cellar.

CHESTER (*moving down R. of the sofa*) Good for Miss Partridge! I
must remember to give her a present. An old skull or
something.

ADA (*crossing to collect her suitcase*) Well, I'd better go and
unpack, I suppose.

CHESTER (*looking at her tiny suitcase*) Yes. You'd better get
started now or you'll never do it by nightfall.

ADA I'm glad you coaxed me, sir.

CHESTER I didn't do that, did I? Well, thank you for your help,
Ada.

ADA Just call for me any time, sir. I'm always ready!

CHESTER Yes, I bet you are.

ADA (*backing towards the archway with the rose*) Goodbye,
sir.

CHESTER Goodbye.

ADA Goodbye, sir!

CHESTER Yes. Rather.

ADA Goodbye!

(*As* ADA *reaches the archway* PATRICIA *comes in.*)

PATRICIA Ada, what on earth are you doing dressed up like that?
And why are you carrying a rose?

ADA I was going off but I'm not any more. He's been coax-
ing me. (*She places the rose in her mouth, growls at*
CHESTER *and goes out.*)

PATRICIA (*moving to C.*) What an extraordinary effect you have
on the servants.

CHESTER (*modestly*) It was nothing, really. She's been helping me.

PATRICIA I'm surprised you needed any help.

CHESTER You see, I was hiding in the wall.

PATRICIA (*doubtfully*) In the wall?

CHESTER Yes—over there.

PATRICIA (*disbelieving*) Really? And what was she doing?

CHESTER She was keeping cave.

PATRICIA With the rose in her mouth.

CHESTER Oh, no. She hadn't got a rose, then.

PATRICIA What a pity.

CHESTER (*moving to her*) You see—those two men were here——

PATRICIA Now, Chester, don't start that again! Nobody the slightest bit suspicious has set foot in the place.

CHESTER But they're here! I saw them!

PATRICIA So you hid in the wall?

CHESTER That's right. Miss Partridge took them into the cellar, and Ada—you know Ada—she knocked on the wall when it was okay for me to come out.

PATRICIA (*to below the armchair*) I'm surprised they didn't find you. (*Sarcastically.*) I mean, everybody hides in the wall, don't they?

CHESTER You don't believe me.

PATRICIA Frankly no.

CHESTER All right, I'll show you! (*To the wall* U.R.C.) If there's one thing I can't stand it's a disbelieving woman. As if I'd make up a thing like that. It's just here. (*He has difficulty in finding the door, laughs.*) Just here. Well, it was here a moment ago. It opened—a door in the wall—opened. (*To L. of the sofa.*) You know how doors open? Well, this one did. Just opened. And closed, of course. It closed afterwards. Funny how you can lose a door. Big thing like that. Silly. I mean, I came out of it and everything —it was a perfectly ordinary door in the wall—you know. I think I need a drink. (*He sits, L. end of the sofa, deflated.*)

PATRICIA It sounds as if you've had too much already.

CHESTER Somehow I thought you'd say that. You mean, you've never had a door in the wall over there?

PATRICIA Not as far as I know.

CHESTER Not even a very little door?

PATRICIA Not even a very little door.

CHESTER Funny. I could have sworn I came through a door.

PATRICIA Perhaps your two friends went out that way. Perhaps that's why we've never seen them.

CHESTER No. They went out through the cellar door. I told you. (*Rising in sudden panic.*) Don't tell me that's gone as well! Oh, no. Still there. Funny how relieved you can be to see a door. They're there all right. They're in the cellar now.

(MAGGIE *and* BERT *walk out from* D.R. *They cross* CHESTER *to* C.)

PATRICIA   Are these the two people you were hiding from?

CHESTER   I don't think so. (*To* MAGGIE *and* BERT.) I say, you're not the——? No, they're not. Very not.

MAGGIE   Strange how alike some of the rooms are in this place, Bert.

BERT   Oh, for 'eaven's sake! We're back 'ere again.

CHESTER   Haven't we met? Haven't I seen you somewhere before?

BERT   Only in passing. You'll be Charles the Second? I'm very pleased to meet you. (*Shakes* CHESTER *by the hand.*) This is Maggie, and I'm Bert.

CHESTER   Maggie and Bert, eh? Dear old M and B. Reminds me of the Army. Have you met Maggie and Bert, darling?

PATRICIA   No.

CHESTER   Well, now's your chance. Maggie, this is Bert. No, that's wrong. Darling, this is Bert. I mean, Bert this is Maggie. Oh, no—you know each other, don't you? Have you seen a door? (*He crosses to* U.R.C.)

PATRICIA   Are you visitors?

BERT   Well, we don't look as if we live 'ere, do we?

PATRICIA   (*crossing to the archway*) Well, if you come along with me we'll find Miss Partridge. She's the guide. She'll show you the way.

BERT   Oh, yes?

(*As* MAGGIE *and* BERT *follow* PATRICIA *there is a loud report offstage.* MAGGIE *and* BERT *react.*)

MAGGIE   What was that?

BERT   Sounded like a shot.

PATRICIA   Yes, it was. That's my father.

MAGGIE   Oh. Out in the garden, shooting at the birds?

PATRICIA   No. Here in the house, shooting at the postman.

BERT   Eh?

PATRICIA   (*reasonably*) Well, it *is* time for the afternoon delivery. (*She goes off through the archway.*)

(*Bemused,* MAGGIE *and* BERT *follow her off.*)

CHESTER   Don't leave me here! All alone—without even a door.

(CHESTER *attempts to find the lost door.* CAPONE *and* WEDGWOOD *come on from the cellar.* CHESTER *does not see them approach. They get near to him.* CAPONE *on his R.,* WEDGWOOD *on his L.*)

CAPONE (*quietly*) Mr. Dreadnought.
(CHESTER *jumps and turns.*)

CHESTER Ah, there you are! I wondered where you'd got to.

CAPONE Won't you sit down, Mr. Dreadnought?

CHESTER That's very civil of you, but as a matter of fact I have to go——

CAPONE (*loudly*) Sit down!

CHESTER Yes. Well, just for a moment, eh? (*He sits on the sofa. They sit either side of him.*) Shall I ring for tea? A few muffins—something like that? How do you like your tea? One each and one for the pot?

CAPONE No.

CHESTER Oh, just one each, then.
(*He starts to rise. They restrain him.*)
No tea?

CAPONE No tea.

CHESTER (*to* WEDGWOOD) How about you?
(WEDGWOOD *shakes his head.*)
Well, I seem to be outvoted. I'll just have to wait. (*Laughs nervously.*)

CAPONE You remember us, Mr. Dreadnought?

CHESTER Of course—how could I forget? You're Mr. Capone. And this is Mr.—er——?

CAPONE Wedgwood.

CHESTER Ah, yes. Wedgwood. I knew it was something delicate. Does he *never* say anything?

CAPONE No.

CHESTER How very relaxing. Well, it's good to see you boys again! How long is it now?

CAPONE Six months.

CHESTER As long as that? Good heavens—it only seems like yesterday.

CAPONE It seemed longer—in prison.

CHESTER In prison? Yes—yes, it would. Cooped up all day—bound to, really.

CAPONE It was a long time—for robbing a little bank.

CHESTER Only a little bank? I thought it was quite a big bank. Quite a nice big bank, really.

CAPONE Was that why you took a photograph of it?

CHESTER I was a street photographer—I took photographs of anything!

CAPONE But just as we happened to be coming out of the bank —with the money?

CHESTER Yes. That was unfortunate, wasn't it?

CAPONE If it had not been for you we might never have gone to prison.

CHESTER No, I suppose not. I'm awfully sorry.

CAPONE So we—we felt we had to come back now—to thank you.

CHESTER Well, that's jolly decent of you. Jolly decent. I'm quite touched.

CAPONE In fact, we would like to do something to repay you.

CHESTER What had you in mind?
(WEDGWOOD *does the grisly mime of removing* CHESTER's *heart, etc.*)
Well, that's very nice of you. But please don't go to any trouble. You've already expressed your gratitude—which I appreciate—and now I'll be off. (*He starts to rise but again is stopped.*)

CAPONE We have not finished yet.

CHESTER Oh. What a pity.

CAPONE That need not happen.

CHESTER What—the—er——? (*Repeats the mime in miniature.*)
Oh, I am relieved!

CAPONE If you help us.

CHESTER Help you? Well, I'm not a very helpful little chap. I'd only be a burden to you. No, no—you're much better on your own.

CAPONE We need your help.

CHESTER To do what?

CAPONE (*rising*) Come over here. (*He takes* CHESTER's R. *arm and leads him towards the fireplace.*)

CHESTER Oh, are we off? (*He turns back to* WEDGWOOD, *who has remained seated.*) Come on! You'll be left behind.
(WEDGWOOD *rises and follows them to face the portrait.*)

CAPONE   What do you think of her?

CHESTER   Who? (*Seeing the portrait.*) Oh—her?

CAPONE   Yes.

CHESTER   Not my type at all. I really prefer a sort of——

CAPONE   We would like to take her with us.

CHESTER   That picture?

CAPONE   Yes.

CHESTER   Whatever for?

CAPONE   She is worth a lot of money, Mr. Dreadnought.

CHESTER   Is she? Go on—you're pulling my leg!

CAPONE   Did you not know?

CHESTER   No, I didn't. And I don't think Lady Elrood does, either.
Are you sure?

CAPONE   Ask Mr. Wedgwood. He is an expert.

CHESTER   Is he? I'd never have known. (*To* WEDGWOOD.) Are you
an expert? (*To* CAPONE.) I mean, he doesn't look like an
expert, does he? Looks more like a bookie.
(WEDGWOOD *turns on him, menacingly.*)
Ah! *now* you look like an expert!

CAPONE   So, Mr. Dreadnought, either you help us to steal this
picture, or else——
(*In unison,* WEDGWOOD *and* CHESTER *do the same business as before.*)
(*To below the sofa.*) Would you like time to think it
over?

CHESTER   Oh, yes, please.

CAPONE   (*turning, after a tiny pause*) The time is up.

CHESTER   What? (*Moving D.C.*) But I've only just started——

CAPONE   What is your decision?

CHESTER   I don't seem to have any choice, do I?

CAPONE   I thought you would see reason.
(*A loud report offstage, and then* LORD ELROOD *charges
on, carrying his shotgun. Sees* CHESTER *and comes to
him.* WEDGWOOD *moves down* R. *of sofa to* R. *of* CAPONE.)

ELROOD   Ah, there you are! Extensive enemy activity in no-
man's-land. Have to watch it. Don't want to leave my
left flank exposed, do I?

CHESTER   Not if you can help it.

ELROOD   Who are these two?

CHESTER   Oh—er—the reinforcements.

ELROOD   Reinforcements, eh? Capital! Capital! (*To* CAPONE.) Well, you ready for a little action?

CAPONE   I am afraid I do not understand.

ELROOD   (*imitating his accent*) 'Understand'? Funny sort of accent for a Britisher. Something damned funny going on here.

CHESTER   I think they're from the other side, sir.

ELROOD   Thought as much! Thought as much! Wouldn't catch a Britisher not at attention before a superior officer. So —we've got a couple of damned enemy spies, eh? (*Points his gun at* CAPONE *and* WEDGWOOD.) Well done, young feller! I'll see you get promotion for this.

CHESTER   Thank you, sir.

ELROOD   (*to* CAPONE) Get 'em up! Get 'em up!
  (CAPONE *and* WEDGWOOD *raise their hands.*)

CAPONE   But we are visitors——

ELROOD   Save it for the trial, eh, lad?

CHESTER   All right if I fall out, sir?

ELROOD   Certainly. Carry on!

CHESTER   Thank you, sir. (*To* CAPONE.) Sorry I can't stay. (*He goes out into the study.*)
  (*The telephone rings.* ELROOD *turns to answer it, and* CAPONE *and* WEDGWOOD *race out after* CHESTER. ELROOD *sees them going.*)

ELROOD   Here, I say! Come back! (*But they have gone.*) Oh, blast! (*Answers the telephone.*) Yes? What is it? What? The grocer? This is a fine time to ring! Don't you know we're in the middle of a war here? (*Slams down the receiver and makes off after* CAPONE *and* WEDGWOOD.) Here! I say! Come back!
  (PATRICIA *comes in from the archway as he races off. The telephone rings again. She answers it.*)

PATRICIA   Hullo? What? What do you mean, 'Is the war over?' (*She shrugs and hangs up.*)
  (CHESTER *races in from the archway. He comes to* R. *of* PATRICIA.)

CHESTER   Darling—quick!

PATRICIA   What is it?

CHESTER   Something's cropped up.

PATRICIA   You've found your door!

CHESTER   No, no! But I spoke to them.

PATRICIA   Who?

CHESTER   Those two men.

PATRICIA   Now, Chester——

CHESTER   It's not really me they're after at all.

PATRICIA   You must be very relieved. (*She starts to go but he stops her and leads her up to below the portrait.*)

CHESTER   It's *her*!

PATRICIA   Who?

CHESTER   Her—up there on the wall!

PATRICIA   (*humouring him*) Oh, I see.

CHESTER   We'll have to move her.

PATRICIA   Why?

CHESTER   Then they won't be able to get her. She'll have to be locked up.

PATRICIA   You're the one who'll have to be locked up.

CHESTER   You don't believe me, do you? That picture's worth a lot of money.

PATRICIA   Don't be silly, darling. Do you think if it was worth anything it wouldn't have been sold by now? Mummy would rather sell a portrait than open up her home to the public.

CHESTER   Perhaps she doesn't know. Come on—give me a hand— we'll take it down and hide it.

PATRICIA   In the wall, I suppose?

CHESTER   What a good idea! If only I could find the door. It would be just the place. They'd never find it there.

PATRICIA   Neither would we.

CHESTER   Are you going to help me or not? I can't do it on my own.

PATRICIA   No, I am not going to help you. And if you attempt to remove that picture I shall telephone the police.

CHESTER   That would be no good.

PATRICIA   Why not?

CHESTER   A wife can't give evidence against her husband.

PATRICIA   If you go on like this it's possible that you may not be my husband for much longer! (*She turns and marches to the archway, meets* ADA *coming in. Angrily:)* What do you want?

ADA Please, miss—there's a Boy Scout in the bathroom.

PATRICIA Oh! (*She marches out.*)

(ADA *approaches* CHESTER, *smiling.*)

ADA She's angry. I heard her.

CHESTER Yes—yes, she is rather.

ADA Maybe you're going to get rid of her, after all? Shall I go and start packing, sir?

CHESTER Packing?

ADA Ready to elope, sir.

CHESTER (*eluding her and moving to below the armchair*) Now, Ada! None of that. I'm still married, you know.

ADA (*with relish*) I don't think it'll take, though, sir. (*She follows to R. of the armchair.*)

CHESTER I say, is there really a Boy Scout in the bathroom?

ADA Yes, sir. The downstairs one. I saw him go in. And there are more of them outside in the garden.

CHESTER Don't tell me there's a coach load come to look at the place?

ADA Looks like it, sir.

(LADY ELROOD *comes down the stairs to below the sofa.*)

LADY E. (*to* ADA) Will you go down and find out what's happening in the garden? Somebody seems to be putting a tent up on the front lawn.

ADA Yes, ma'am. (*Turning at the archway.*) I expect it's them.

LADY E. Them?

ADA The Boy Scouts. (*She goes.*)

LADY E. What on earth is the girl talking about?

CHESTER She says there's one in the bathroom.

LADY E. A Boy Scout?

CHESTER Yes.

LADY E. I can't understand what's going on.

(LORD ELROOD *returns disgruntled, crossing to the stairs R.*)

ELROOD Damned fellows gave me the slip.

CHESTER Oh, no! (*He makes for the panel door* U.R.C.)

LADY E. Darling, tea will be here soon. You will come and have some, won't you?

ELROOD I lose two prisoners of war and you offer me tea!

LADY E. It's so long since you sat down and had tea. You haven't had crumpets for ages.

ELROOD Crumpets? Hate 'em! (*He reaches the foot of the stairs and starts up them.*)

LADY E. With all these visitors about I do think they ought to be able to see us enjoying afternoon tea. It's what they expect somehow. We might even invite some of them to join us.

ELROOD Are you mad?

LADY E. I thought it would be a nice touch.

ELROOD It's a ghastly touch! (*He goes off.*)

(CHESTER *is trying to find the panel door.* LADY ELROOD *moves up to below the fireplace.*)

LADY E. What are you looking for, dear?

CHESTER Oh, nothing, really. Only a door. You haven't seen one, have you? About here, it was. I'm rather anxious to find it.

LADY E. Oh—that door!

CHESTER (*delighted*) You know about it?

LADY E. Of course I know about it. It used to be in that wall somewhere.

CHESTER Used to be?

LADY E. We haven't seen it for ages. It leads into the library.

CHESTER Yes, I know. That's the way I found it.

LADY E. (*logically*) Well, then, go into the library and come through that way.

CHESTER No good. I tried. I can't find the door in the library either.

(*The panel door creaks open.*)

CHESTER }(*together*) There it is!
LADY E. }

(CAPONE *and* WEDGWOOD *emerge.* WEDGWOOD *closes the door behind them.*)

CHESTER I must be off! (*He runs off through the study door.*)

(CAPONE *bows to* LADY ELROOD.)

CAPONE Good afternoon.

LADY E. Oh—good afternoon.

(CAPONE *nudges* WEDGWOOD, *who quickly doffs his hat*

and bows. Then they both turn and rush off after CHESTER.)
What delightful manners.
(LADY ELROOD *crosses to below the sofa.* ADA *comes in from the hall.*)

ADA   Mr. Willis!
   (*She withdraws and* GEORGE WILLIS *comes in. He is a solid, enthusiastic man of about 40 in the uniform of a Scoutmaster. He comes in to C.*)

LADY E.   Good heavens! What are you?

GEORGE   Willis.

LADY E.   Willis?

GEORGE   George Willis—at your service. (*He salutes, Boy Scout fashion.*)

LADY E.   Aren't you a little old to be a Boy Scout?

GEORGE   I'm a master.

LADY E.   Schoolmaster?

GEORGE   Scoutmaster.

LADY E.   Oh, I see. It wasn't you, was it?

GEORGE   I beg your pardon?

LADY E.   In the downstairs one.

GEORGE   Downstairs?

LADY E.   Bathroom.

GEORGE   Oh. No.

LADY E.   Not you?

GEORGE   Oh, no.

LADY E.   Was that you on the lawn?

GEORGE   I was on the lawn, yes.

LADY E.   Putting up a tent?

GEORGE   It was the first.

LADY E.   I don't think I know what you're talking about.

GEORGE   We always put that one up first.

LADY E.   Oh, do you?

GEORGE   Then the others take their position from that.

LADY E.   I see. Tell me—how many boys are there?

GEORGE   About fifty.

LADY E.   You don't sound very certain.

GEORGE   Well, it was fifty at the last count.

LADY E.   All outside.

GEORGE All outside. Except for the one in the downstairs——

LADY E. Precisely. (*Pleased.*) And you all want to look around the house? (*Moving slightly R.*) Well, let's see, fifty at half price will be fifty times one and three plus one adult——

GEORGE Er—Lady Elrood——

LADY E. (*turning to face him*) About three pounds five, I think—

GEORGE (*moving down level with her*) Lady Elrood—you're wrong——

LADY E. Well, I *think* it's three pounds five—let me see——

GEORGE We don't want to look over the house.

LADY E. You don't?

GEORGE No.

LADY E. Then may I ask what you're doing here?

GEORGE Camping.

LADY E. I beg your pardon?

GEORGE In the garden.

LADY E. In my garden?

GEORGE Yes. That was the first of the tents going up.

LADY E. And how many more do you intend putting up?

GEORGE Another six—and one for the catering.

LADY E. That's eight in all?

GEORGE Correct!

LADY E. All on my lawn?

GEORGE It's an ideal site.

LADY E. I'm sure it is.

GEORGE You've kept it beautifully, Lady Elrood.

LADY E. I needn't have bothered, need I?

GEORGE Oh, we'll clear up everything when we leave.

LADY E. And relay the turf, I assume?

GEORGE (*laughing*) Well, we couldn't go quite as far as that, now, could we? (*His laugh dies gradually as he sees her set expression.*)

LADY E. (*to him*) Mr. Willis—troop leader—Boy Scout manager—whatever you may be called—are you aware of the fact that you are trespassing?

GEORGE Oh, no.

LADY E. (*crossing him to the telephone*) Oh, *yes*, Mr. Willis. You and your boys—all fifty of them—are trespassing in

my garden and on my lawn, and unless I have a completely satisfactory explanation within the next thirty
seconds I shall telephone the police. (*She looks at her
watch.*)

GEORGE (*staring at her, aghast*) Well, really, Lady Elrood—I'm
a little surprised at your attitude.

LADY E. Are you? Are you aware, Mr. Willis, that this land
is private property?

GEORGE Yes, of course.

LADY E. Well, I'm glad you admit that. Your time is up. I shall
telephone the police. (*She lifts the receiver.*)

GEORGE But you gave us permission!

LADY E. What did you say?

GEORGE We wrote to you. Don't you remember?

LADY E. I certainly do not.

GEORGE About six months ago. Had a charming letter back
saying we could camp in your garden this week-end—
so here we are.

(LADY ELROOD *replaces the receiver.*)

LADY E. I need hardly tell you, Mr. Willis, that I never wrote
such a letter.

GEORGE Well, somebody did. I've got the letter here, as a matter
of fact. (*He produces a letter.*) There we are.

(LADY ELROOD *takes the letter, crosses below* GEORGE *to
the sofa and reads it. She looks up towards the stairs.*)

LADY E. (*quietly*) I shall kill him. I shall kill him with my bare
hands.

GEORGE It is in order, you see, Lady Elrood.

LADY E. (*taking the letter back to* GEORGE) I regret to say, it is.
That letter was written by my husband. (*Crossing to
D.L.*) Oh, but this is dreadful! We can't have hordes
of Boy Scouts all over the place.

GEORGE I'm afraid you've got them. It'll only be for two days.

LADY E. Two days! Fifty Boy Scouts trampling on my flower
beds and monopolising the lavatory? It's unthinkable.

GEORGE Well, I'm afraid it's too late to change our plans now,
Lady Elrood.

LADY E. I don't know what I've done to deserve this. I have to
open my house to the public to raise funds to pay the

grocer, my husband is shooting at the postman, my son-in-law is behaving like a lunatic—and now I've got Boy Scouts in the back garden! It's too much!

(MISS PARTRIDGE *comes in from the cellar to below the sofa.*)

MISS P.   There's a crowd of small boys in the garden.

LADY E.   Yes, Miss Partridge, we know. They're Boy Scouts.

MISS P.   Oh, I wondered why they had those dear little hats on. (*Sees* GEORGE.) Oh! Here's a bigger one!

LADY E.   This is Mr. Willis. They belong to him.

MISS P.   All of them? Well, well! I suppose it's all that fresh air you get. (*To* LADY E.) You haven't seen my visitors, have you? I've lost some. As soon as I begin to show people around they seem to disappear. Twice I've been left alone in the cellar talking to myself.

(PATRICIA *enters from the archway to above the arm-chair.*)

PATRICIA   Mummy, there are tents all over the front lawn!

LADY E.   (*wearily*) Yes, dear—we know!

PATRICIA   Well, whatever's going on? (*Reacts and turns to look at* GEORGE.)

GEORGE   (*weakly*) We're just putting them up.

PATRICIA   (*bemused*) Mummy?

LADY E.   You heard what he said. They're putting them up!

PATRICIA   Why?

LADY E.   (*crossly*) Well, we can't have them all sleeping in here, can we?

GEORGE   (*smiling*) Well, that might not be a bad——

LADY E.   Please, Mr. Willis, get back to your boys.

GEORGE   Yes—yes, rather. Better see how they're getting on. Thank you for being so understanding, Lady Elrood. We won't leave a mess. Scout's honour!

(*He salutes and goes out through the archway.* PATRICIA *watches him go, bemused.*)

PATRICIA   Where did he come from?

LADY E.   I don't know! Where do Boy Scouts come from? I think I'm going to faint.

PATRICIA   (*to her quickly*) Mummy, darling——

LADY E.   I need tea—buckets of steaming hot tea, or I shall die!

PATRICIA   It'll be here soon. (*Leading her towards the stairs.*) Come
           along, you have a lie down until it's ready. You'll soon
           be all right.

LADY E.   I shall have tea and then I shall kill him.

PATRICIA   Who?

LADY E.   Your father. I shall shoot him with his own gun. He
           shall pay for it! He shall pay for it. I promise you!
           (*They go off upstairs.* MISS PARTRIDGE *is watching them
           go, a little surprised, as the panel door creaks open and*
           CAPONE *and* WEDGWOOD *appear. She goes up to below
           the fireplace.*)

MISS P.   There you are, boys! I've been looking for you every-
           where! I was just going to show you the Norman relics,
           I believe. Most fascinating.

CAPONE   Well, we are a little tired at the moment. We thought
           a rest here perhaps. My friend is not very strong.

MISS P.   I am sorry. Poor fellow. Well, while you're resting, per-
           haps I could tell you a little of the history of the West
           Wing—— (*She starts to get out her guide book.*)

CAPONE   Oh, I think I saw those other two people looking for
           you in the library. They were very anxious to find
           you.

MISS P.   I forgot all about them! I am remiss. You'll have to
           excuse me, then. Now, don't go away. I don't want to
           lose you again. I shall be back.

CAPONE   We will be here.

MISS P.   Splendid! (*She goes hurriedly out through the archway.*)

CAPONE   Quickly!
           (WEDGWOOD *runs to the hall door, looks out, returns.*)
           All clear?
           (WEDGWOOD *nods.*)
           Good. We must work quickly. We will put her in here
           for the moment.
           (*Carefully and with difficulty they take down the portrait
           from above the fireplace. It is very heavy.* WEDGWOOD
           almost drops his side.)
           Careful!
           (*They proceed. A noise off.*)
           Somebody coming! Quickly!

(They quickly take the portrait out through the panel door, closing it behind them. CHESTER *comes on from the archway. He peers this way and that for* CAPONE *and* WEDGWOOD, *but does not notice that the portrait has gone. Satisfied that nobody is there he goes to sit and relax, looks at the empty space as he passes, sits and then reacts. He jumps up.)*

CHESTER It's gone! It's gone! They've got it! *(Racing for the archway.)* Pat! Darling—where are you? *(He goes off.)*

*(*CAPONE *and* WEDGWOOD *emerge with the portrait.)*

CAPONE Quickly!

*(*WEDGWOOD *goes to the archway, looks out as before and returns.)*

All clear?

*(*WEDGWOOD *nods.* CAPONE *closes the panel door and they carry the portrait to the archway.* CAPONE *looks out, returns in panic. The rattle of a tea-trolley can be heard.)*

The maid!

(They rush back to the panel door. WEDGWOOD *tries to open it but cannot do so.)*

Quick! Quick! Can't you find it?

*(*WEDGWOOD *shakes his head in panic.* CAPONE *tries, also fails. Outside we hear the rattle of the approaching tea-trolley. In panic they return the portrait to its position on the wall and race out D.R. as* ADA *comes in from the hall, pushing a tea-trolley noisily. She brings it to L. of the sofa.)*

ADA Tea! *(Sees nobody there.)* Well, I don't care if it gets cold. *(She takes a biscuit and makes for the archway.)*

(As she reaches the archway, LADY ELROOD *and* PATRICIA *come downstairs.)*

LADY E. Is tea ready, Jessica?

ADA Ada! Over there! *(She goes out, eating the biscuit.)*

LADY E. I wish we could find a nice quiet girl. It would make such a difference. Oh, my head! *(Sits in the armchair.)*

PATRICIA *(busy at the trolley)* Have some tea, Mummy. You'll soon feel better.

LADY E. But what are we going to do? I mean, two or three Boy

Scouts might be rather nice. A bob a job and all that. But fifty is really going too far.

PATRICIA Perhaps Daddy will think of something. (*She brings a chair down to L. of the trolley.*)

LADY E. That's hardly likely, is it? Your father hasn't thought of anything sensible for thirty years.
(MAGGIE *and* BERT *come in from the study. They see* LADY ELROOD *and* PATRICIA *having tea and are a little embarrassed.*)

MAGGIE Oh, I'm ever so sorry. We didn't know you were 'aving tea. I'm afraid we've got a bit lost.

LADY E. (*a little long-suffering*) That's quite all right. Do come in. Perhaps you'd care to join us?

MAGGIE (*amazed*) Have tea with you, your ladyship?

LADY E. Why not?

MAGGIE Well, that's awfully kind of you. What do you say, Bert?

BERT What's it going to cost?

MAGGIE Bert!

LADY E. It won't cost you anything, Mr.—er———?

BERT Well, that's all right, then. 'Cos I've paid out enough already, see?

LADY E. Do sit down.

MAGGIE Thank you, your ladyship.
(MAGGIE *crosses to the sofa, bobbing a curtsy to* LADY ELROOD *as she passes.* BERT *does likewise. They sit, side by side, on the sofa. She is subdued, he belligerent. He does not remove his cap. She nudges him.*)
(*Quietly*) Bert!

BERT What is it?

MAGGIE (*quietly*) Your cap.

BERT Eh?

MAGGIE (*quietly*) Take your cap off!
(BERT *removes his cap but does not know where to put it. Eventually puts it over the muffin dish on the R. end of the trolley.* PATRICIA *gives a cup of tea to* MAGGIE. LADY ELROOD *takes a cup for herself and resumes her seat.*)
Oh, thank you.

PATRICIA Sugar?

MAGGIE Yes, please. (*Takes sugar.*)
    (PATRICIA *hands a cup of tea to* BERT.)
BERT Ta.
PATRICIA Sugar?
BERT Yes. (*Takes rather a lot.*) Lumps, eh? Never 'ave these at 'ome. (*Takes a handful and puts it in his pocket.*) Ta.
PATRICIA Now—who'd like a crumpet?
MAGGIE That would be very nice, your ladyship.
PATRICIA Yes. (*She cannot find the crumpets.*) Yes, it would. I'm sure I saw crumpets here a moment ago.
    (MAGGIE *sees* BERT'S *cap.*)
MAGGIE (*in a whisper*) Bert!
BERT What's up?
MAGGIE Your cap.
BERT Eh?
MAGGIE Take your cap off the table!
    (*He retrieves his cap.*)
PATRICIA Ah, there they are! (*Busies herself with the crumpets.*)
    (BERT *is undecided, cap in one hand, cup in the other.* PATRICIA *passes a plate with a crumpet on it to* MAGGIE, *then offers one to* BERT. *He has no free hand, so after a moment's hesitation puts the cap down the front of his coat and takes the plate. Now both* MAGGIE *and* BERT *can neither eat nor drink, both having a cup in one hand and a plate in the other. Business ad lib. Meantime,* LADY ELROOD *and* PATRICIA *drink tea and eat, oblivious of the difficulties.*
    MAGGIE *puts her plate on top of* BERT'S *cup, takes a drink of tea and takes the plate back again.* BERT, *suffering agonies, puts his plate on top of his own cup, puts a piece of crumpet in his mouth. The cup is suddenly in danger and he retrieves the plate, leaving the crumpet in his mouth.*)
    Another crumpet, Mr——? (*She sees his predicament.*)
    (*He shakes his head, the crumpet between his lips wobbles. With a deft jerk of the head he throws the crumpet up in the air and catches it on his plate.*)
    Shall I take your cup, Mr——?
    (*He nods his head. She takes his cup and puts it on the*

*tray. BERT then copes with his crumpet. MAGGIE attempts
to keep face.)*
Another crumpet?

BERT No fear. I mean—no thank you.

PATRICIA Then have a cake.

BERT Ta. Don't mind if I do. 'Ow about you, Maggie?

*(He puts a cake on top of the crumpet on MAGGIE's plate.
She has still got the plate in one hand and her cup in
the other. He puts a cake on his own plate, a cream
cake with a rather hard pastry shell. PATRICIA gives him
a fork. He is uncertain, glances at MAGGIE, then leans
across and stirs her tea with it. She glares. He then sees
PATRICIA using a fork and decides to do the same. He
tries to hoist the whole cake towards his mouth, balanced
on the fork. The cake eludes him and shoots off the plate
like a bullet, missing LADY ELROOD by a hairsbreadth.
He gets up and pursues it as LORD ELROOD charges down
the stairs.)*

ELROOD *(seeing BERT on all fours at LADY ELROOD's feet)* What
are you doing down there?

BERT *(looking up)* I'm picking up my cake.

ELROOD This is no time for cake, man! I shall expect you and
your men at action stations in two minutes. The enemy
are in sight. I recognised their uniforms. About fifty of
the blighters out there already.

LADY E. *(with menace)* Yes—I wanted to speak to you about
that, dear.

*(BERT returns to sofa and continues to try to eat cake,
hindered by the fork.)*

PATRICIA *(quickly)* Daddy, do have some tea.

ELROOD Good idea. *(He takes the cup and the plate of food from
the astonished MAGGIE and goes off.)*

LADY E. *(rising hurriedly to follow him)* Darling, just a moment.
(To MAGGIE.) You will excuse me a moment, won't you?
(She follows ELROOD off.) There was something I wanted
to talk to you about. *(Exit.)*

MAGGIE Who was that?

PATRICIA That's my father.

MAGGIE Oh, I am sorry, dear.

(CHESTER *comes in from the archway. He does not see that the portrait is back.*)

CHESTER (*moving to* PATRICIA) Well—you're looking very calm, darling.

PATRICIA Why shouldn't I be calm?

CHESTER (*noticing* MAGGIE *and* BERT) Because of—good afternoon —because of what's happened!

PATRICIA What has happened?

CHESTER (*waving a finger at her playfully*) You didn't believe me, did you? Oh, no!

PATRICIA Believe you?

CHESTER I bet you had a pang of conscience when you saw it.

PATRICIA Saw it?

CHESTER Don't tell me you haven't seen it?

PATRICIA Not a thing.

CHESTER (*taking her hand and leading her to the portrait*) Well, come and have a look and then you can apologise. There you are, you see—what did I tell you? (*He sees the portrait is there.*) It's there!

PATRICIA Of course it's there.

CHESTER It wasn't a moment ago.

PATRICIA Now, darling, portraits don't come and go like that.

CHESTER This one did. I came in through that door and there it wasn't. Just a space, that's all—just a clean mark on the wall! You've seen a clean mark on a wall! Well, that's what this was. No portrait—just a mark on a wall!

(MAGGIE *and* BERT, *ignored on the sofa, pull the tea trolley across in front of them and settle gratefully into the food.*)

PATRICIA Darling, pull yourself together. You were mistaken, that's all.

CHESTER I was not mistaken! I tell you there was no portrait there—it had gone—they'd taken it!

PATRICIA If they'd taken it why should they put it back?

CHESTER How should I know?

(BERT *is again experimenting with the cake fork.*)

PATRICIA Darling, I'm getting a little tired. First of all you start looking for a non-existent door in a wall——

CHESTER It does exist!

PATRICIA —and now you start imagining stupid things about a portrait.

CHESTER But it's true! It had disappeared!

PATRICIA Darling—it's there!

CHESTER I know it's there *now*, blast it! But it wasn't there then! (BERT *abandons the fork and eats with his fingers.*)

PATRICIA I expect you'll tell me next that it got down off the wall all by itself, had a walk about the room and got back up again?

CHESTER Oh darling, a portrait can't walk. Don't be silly. (MAGGIE *considers the plate of cakes.*)

PATRICIA I'm going!

CHESTER Going?

PATRICIA If you haven't pulled yourself together in five minutes I shall leave!

CHESTER Leave? Because a portrait went and came back again?

PATRICIA Because I can't stand any more of your nonsense! (MAGGIE *slides the cakes off the plate into her handbag.* PATRICIA *makes for the archway.* GEORGE *comes in, carrying a bucket.*)

GEORGE I say, could I have a bucket of water?

PATRICIA Ooh! (*She storms past him and goes.*) (LORD ELROOD *appears at the top of the stairs. He sees* GEORGE.)

ELROOD Good heavens! There's one of 'em inside! (*He races down the stairs and across towards* GEORGE *with his gun at the ready. The astonished* GEORGE *is making his escape and* MAGGIE *is pouring* BERT *some more tea as——*

THE CURTAIN FALLS

ACT III

The same evening.
When the curtain rises GEORGE *looks in through the archway. He is carrying a bucket and has his hat in his hand.*

GEORGE (*tentatively*) I say—is anybody there?
(*He comes into the room, looking about. As he gets* C. *a loud report is heard from offstage. He reacts.* LORD ELROOD *comes down the stairs.*)

ELROOD Missed again, blast it! Damn fellow's too quick for me. Zig-zagging all the time.

GEORGE Who, sir?

ELROOD Fellow in a uniform.

GEORGE Oh, that'll be the postman. I saw him running up the drive just now.

ELROOD He ran down it a damn sight quicker! (*To below the sofa.*)

GEORGE You mean you've been shooting at him?

ELROOD The fellow's a spy. Still, scattered a few of the enemy while I was about it.

GEORGE (*in horror*) The enemy?

ELROOD Encamped on the lawn. Ha! Ha! Little blighters! You should have seen 'em run for cover! (*He laughs mercilessly.*)

GEORGE (*protesting*) Now, Lord Elrood, I must point out——

ELROOD (*recognising him*) Here—I say—it's *you* again! Didn't recognise you without your lid on. Get 'em up! (*Waves his shotgun under* GEORGE's *nose.*)

GEORGE (*raising his hands*) Lord Elrood, I must explain——

ELROOD What are you doing here, eh? What's your purpose?

GEORGE I came to get water.

ELROOD Why? Is the place on fire?

GEORGE No, sir.

ELROOD Then what do you want water for?

GEORGE. Tea, sir. For the boys.

ELROOD Ah! I'm so sorry. Didn't realise. You're the cook
sergeant. You should have said. Ring the bell. The
maid'll see to you. I must get back to the men. (*Con-
fidentially.*) Big counter-offensive to-night. (*Going.*) Keep
it under your hat.

GEORGE Yes, of course. (*He puts his hat back on hastily.*)
(ELROOD *goes off upstairs.* ADA *comes in, angrily, from
the archway.*)

ADA Who's got my bucket? (*Sees* GEORGE, *who has nervously
put the bucket behind him.*) You're still here, then?
(*Starts to laugh.*)

GEORGE What's the matter?

ADA I can't get over your knees!

GEORGE What do you mean?

ADA Well, they don't seem to belong to you, do they? You
know—they act sort of on their own—as if they didn't
want anything to do with the rest of you.

GEORGE Now, look here——

ADA (*angry again*) 'Ere! You've got it!

GEORGE What?

ADA My bucket.

GEORGE This is *my* bucket.

ADA Oh no it's not.

GEORGE Oh yes it is.

ADA Where would you get a bucket from?

GEORGE I brought it with me. *This* bucket.

ADA Well, my bucket's gone. Someone's removed my bucket
from its quarters.

GEORGE It's not me. This has always been my bucket.

ADA (*moving in*) Are you going to give it to me?

GEORGE No, I certainly am not. I need this bucket for tea.

ADA And I need it for mopping down the floor, so give it here!
(ADA *grabs the bucket but* GEORGE *will not part with it.
They struggle, below the sofa.*)
Give me my bucket!

GEORGE My bucket!

ADA   Mine!

GEORGE Mine!

(CHESTER *comes in through the archway as they are struggling and watches them, R. of the armchair.*)

CHESTER I'm not interrupting anything, am I?

(*They stop struggling.*)

ADA   (*hurt*) I just came to get my bucket.

CHESTER Quite right, too. Go on, Mr. Willis, give her what she's asking for.

(GEORGE *glares at him.*)

Her bucket. She's got work to do. She can't stay here playing about with you all day.

(GEORGE *reluctantly hands over the bucket.* ADA *takes it, glares at* GEORGE *and turns to beam at* CHESTER.)

ADA   Thank you, sir. I always said you were a gentleman. (*She goes.*)

(CHESTER *turns to look at* GEORGE, *who cowers, embarrassed.*)

CHESTER I'm surprised at you. I come in casually and find you struggling with a bucket.

GEORGE It was the maid.

CHESTER Yes—the maid *and* the bucket. What were you up to?

GEORGE Trying to get it.

CHESTER Trying to get it? You stand there—your knees all bare —and say you were trying to get it?

GEORGE It's my bucket.

CHESTER I don't care whose bucket it is. It was a nasty struggle. Very nasty. If I hadn't come in when I did heaven knows what would have happened.

GEORGE I'd have got it!

CHESTER I don't doubt that. (*To below the armchair.*) What would those boys out there think if they knew you were up here struggling with a helpless female? You'd never look Ralph Reader in the eye again.

GEORGE Why should I give away my bucket?

CHESTER How do you know it was yours? Did you mark your bucket?

GEORGE Of course not.

CHESTER Then how do you know it's yours?

GEORGE   (*crossly*) I've had it a long time and I know what it looks like!

CHESTER   You can't say that about a bucket. A wife, yes. Or a greenhouse. Perhaps it wasn't just the bucket you were after?

GEORGE   What do you mean by that?

CHESTER   It was a nasty struggle. Rather nastier than the average man would have over a bucket.

GEORGE   What are you suggesting?

CHESTER   I'm suggesting that all this flapdoodle about a bucket is really a cover up for your deeper intention.

GEORGE   You don't mean——?

CHESTER   Yes, that's exactly what I do mean!

GEORGE   You know that's not true.

CHESTER   (*crossing slowly to* L. *of* GEORGE) Oh, yes. I know it's not true. And you know it's not true. But nobody else knows it's not true.

GEORGE   You wouldn't——?

CHESTER   I might. (*With a sudden smile.*) But not if you help me.

GEORGE   (*doubtfully*) Help you?

CHESTER   To take down that picture.

GEORGE   Why?

CHESTER   It's too heavy to do on my own.

GEORGE   I mean, why do you want to take it down?

CHESTER   It's a long story.

GEORGE   I'll wait.

CHESTER   It's longer than that. There isn't time. It's got to be done now. You want to do your good deed, don't you?

GEORGE   Well, I——

CHESTER   Oh, come on! I'll give you a bob afterwards. (*He pulls* GEORGE *upstage.*)

GEORGE   But I don't understand——

CHESTER   You don't have to. Just remember—you'll be doing Lady Elrood a favour. You want to do her a favour, don't you?

GEORGE   Well, I——

CHESTER   After all, if she heard about you and the maid carrying on in here——

GEORGE   We weren't carrying on!

CHESTER   Well, whatever it was—if she heard about it she might stop you camping on the lawn.

GEORGE   Oh, very well! But I wish I knew why we're doing it.

CHESTER   I'll tell you later. Come on.
            (*They start to get the portrait off the wall.*)
            Ready?

GEORGE   Yes.

CHESTER   Right. Here we go.
            (MISS PARTRIDGE *comes in from the cellar. She sees them.*)

MISS P.   Can I help you?

CHESTER   No, no—that's quite all right. You run along. I think you're wanted in the library.

MISS P.   I hope I find them this time. (*She wanders out through the archway.*)

CHESTER   Come on—quickly!

GEORGE   She's a bit heavy, isn't she?

CHESTER   Well, you know these rich ladies. Too much food and not enough exercise. Over here.
            (*They get the portrait to the middle of the room as* LADY ELROOD *and* PATRICIA *come in from the study. They come to* L. *of* CHESTER *and stop aghast at what they see.*)

LADY E.   What on earth's going on?

CHESTER   (*turning to* GEORGE) Yes!—what on earth's going on, George?

GEORGE   Don't ask me!

PATRICIA   What are you doing with that picture, Chester?

CHESTER   Nothing now.

PATRICIA   What's it doing there?

CHESTER   I was looking at it. I like looking at pictures.

PATRICIA   Did you have to get it down to look at it?

CHESTER   I'm short-sighted.

LADY E.   You know what this looks like to me?

CHESTER   (*peering at the portrait*) It's a lady, isn't it?

LADY E.   I don't like the look of it at all.

CHESTER   Oh, I thought it was rather a nice face.

LADY E.   I'm waiting!

CHESTER   Are you? For long?

LADY E.   For an explanation.

CHESTER   Ah, yes. Well, he can.

LADY E. Who can?

CHESTER Go on, George, give them a long explanation.

GEORGE But I never——!

LADY E. It looks to me like theft!

CHESTER And that's not all! If I hadn't come in when I did heaven knows what would have happened.

PATRICIA Chester!

CHESTER Yes, dear?

PATRICIA What were you doing with the picture?

CHESTER Yes—the picture. Well, you see, somebody's trying to steal it.

LADY E. I can see that!

CHESTER Oh, not us.

LADY E. No?

CHESTER Those two men—the ones I told you about. You see, it's worth a lot of money, and they're trying to steal it. So we thought we'd beat them to it.

LADY E. And steal it first?

CHESTER And steal it first. No! Not steal it. We thought we'd put it away for safe keeping until they'd gone.

LADY E. I've a good mind to call the police.

CHESTER Oh, don't do that. (To GEORGE.) We don't want her to do that, do we?

LADY E. But as you are now—unhappily—my blood relation, I'll give you another chance.

CHESTER But it's true——

LADY E. Put that picture back where you found it, and I shall say no more about it.

CHESTER But those two men——

LADY E. If you have not put it back within two minutes I shall telephone the police, son-in-law or no son-in-law! Come, Patricia!

(She and PATRICIA march out through the archway.)

CHESTER You see what happens? You try to help somebody and all they do is snarl and sneer. Sneer and snarl, all the time. It's demoralising.

GEORGE Are you sure somebody's trying to steal it?

CHESTER Of course I am. They told me.

GEORGE Told you?

CHESTER   Yes.

GEORGE   Doesn't sound very likely.

CHESTER   I know it doesn't, but it's true.

GEORGE   Then why don't you tell the police?

CHESTER   They wouldn't believe me any more than she does.

GEORGE   Well, there's nothing you can do. If we don't put it back now she'll call the police.

CHESTER   Yes, I suppose so. Come on, then.
          (*They take the portrait back to the wall.*)
          All right?

GEORGE   Yes.

CHESTER   Up we go.
          (*They put the portrait back on the wall.*)
          We'll have to think of something else.

GEORGE   Not me. I've got to get back to my boys. (*Makes for the archway.*)

CHESTER   Now, George, you wouldn't leave me to face this alone?

GEORGE   Yes, I would! I've got fifty hungry boys to see to. Oh, and by the way—you owe me a shilling. (*He goes.*)
          (CHESTER *looks thoughtfully at the portrait. The panel door creaks open slowly. He turns to see* CAPONE *and* WEDGWOOD *emerging and runs in panic to the archway.*)
          George! George—wait for me! (*He goes.*)
          (WEDGWOOD *makes to follow* CHESTER, *but* CAPONE *stops him and shakes his head. They go back through the panel door and bring out another portrait the same size as the one on the wall.*)

CAPONE   Quick! (*Jerks his head towards the archway.*)
          (WEDGWOOD *goes and looks out, shakes his head and returns to C. They quickly get down the portrait of the lady from the wall and lean it against the sofa.*)
          We will cover up the mark with this one, h'm?
          (WEDGWOOD *nods enthusiastically. They start to put the second portrait up. It is a picture of a horse's head. A sudden noise off.*)
          Somebody coming!
          (*They freeze either side of the portrait and remain absolutely still.* MISS PARTRIDGE *comes in from the archway.*)

MISS P. Anybody there? (*She moves into the room.*) I wonder where they've all got to. (*She looks casually and sees the portrait of the horse flanked by* CAPONE *and* WEDGWOOD, *but moves on without reacting. Then she stops below the sofa, thinks, looks back, thinks again, does not believe her eyes and goes off into the cellar* D.R.)
(CAPONE *and* WEDGWOOD *finish putting up the new portrait and then pick up the one of the lady.*)

CAPONE We will put her in here for the time being.
(*They put the portrait out through the panel door, close the door and go off* R. LADY ELROOD *and* PATRICIA *return.*)

LADY E. If he hasn't put it back I promise you I shall telephone the police.

PATRICIA Give him another chance, Mummy, please. He's very overwrought.
(LADY ELROOD *sees a portrait on the wall but does not react to what it is. They sit down,* LADY ELROOD *on the sofa,* PATRICIA *in the armchair.*)

LADY E. Ah, good! I hoped I could trust him.

PATRICIA I knew all along that he'd put it back.
(*They subside into silence and react slowly to what they have seen. They look first at each other, and then in unison towards the portrait. They make a concerted rush up to below the portrait.*)

LADY E. What—on—earth—is—that?

PATRICIA I think it's a horse, Mummy.

LADY E. I know it's a horse, but what's it doing there?

PATRICIA I don't know.

LADY E. (*exploding*) What's he done to my picture? What's he done to it?. (*Crossing to below the armchair.*) I shall kill him for this! I shall kill him!

PATRICIA (*following to* L. *of the armchair*) Perhaps he can explain——

LADY E. I'd like to know how he's going to explain a horse on the wall! (*She sinks into the armchair.*)
(CHESTER *comes in from the archway. He moves to* R. *of the armchair.*)

CHESTER (*cheerfully*) Well, there you are, you see—I did it!

LADY E. (*grimly*) You did it, all right.

CHESTER (*playfully*) And you were so suspicious! Fancy suspect-
         ing me like that. No faith, that's your trouble. No faith
         at all.

LADY E. Where—is—it?

CHESTER H'm?

LADY E. Where is my portrait?

CHESTER It's there—I put it back—it's on the wall.

LADY E. (*rising imperiously*) Look at it!

CHESTER What about it?

LADY E. It's a horse!

CHESTER Are you feeling all right?

LADY E. It's a horse!

CHESTER A horse?

LADY E. Yes—look at it!

CHESTER It was a lady before.

LADY E. It's a horse now.

CHESTER But that's impossible.

LADY E. Look at it, man! Look at it!
         (CHESTER *moves to L. of the sofa and looks at the
         portrait for a time.*)
         Well? Well?

CHESTER That's a horse all right. A big brown horse.

LADY E. The colour is immaterial.

CHESTER I thought you'd like to know I was observant. I've always
         been an observant little chap.

LADY E. How do you explain it?

CHESTER The lady, you mean?

LADY E. The horse!

CHESTER Yes—the lady and the horse. (*He comes downstage
         again.*) She must have changed.

LADY E. Changed?

CHESTER Into a horse.

LADY E. A picture can't change.

CHESTER I suppose it *was* a lady? I mean, we might have been
         mistaken. At a quick glance, in a bad light—you know.

LADY E. (*patiently*) It was a lady.

CHESTER (*thoughtfully*) Maybe she was sitting on a horse. That
         would account for it.

LADY E. How?

CHESTER   Maybe she had to go away. Left the horse behind. She'll be back in a minute.

LADY E.   She was not sitting on a horse!

CHESTER   What was she sitting on?

LADY E.   Nothing.

CHESTER   Sitting on nothing?

LADY E.   As far as I know.

CHESTER   Ah! But how far do you know?

LADY E.   It was a head and shoulders, that's all. A head and shoulders.

CHESTER   Well, she might still have been on a horse—lower down.

LADY E.   There was no horse in the picture!

CHESTER   There is now.

LADY E.   What are you going to do about it?

CHESTER   Why? Don't you like horses?

LADY E.   I'm waiting for a sensible explanation. Why don't you say something?

CHESTER   I can't think of anything.

LADY E.   That's what I thought. (*She makes for the stairs.*)

CHESTER   Where are you going?

LADY E.   I'm going to find my husband. He'll know how to deal with you! (*She goes up the stairs.*)

CHESTER   You mustn't tell him!

LADY E.   Why not?

CHESTER   He'll reduce me to the ranks.

(LADY ELROOD *goes off.* CHESTER *moves to* PATRICIA D.L.C.)

PATRICIA   Darling—what is going on?

CHESTER   I wish I knew. You've got to believe me. I've never seen that horse before in my life.

PATRICIA   I expect it was amongst all that old rubbish in the cellar. There are lots of pictures down there. But why is it on the wall?

CHESTER   I don't know, darling.

PATRICIA   And where is the other picture—the one you say is worth so much money?

CHESTER   I don't know that either. When you went out just now, old George and I put the lady back up on the wall— and that's the last I saw of her! I swear to you.

PATRICIA Oh, dear. I want to think you're telling me the truth.

CHESTER (*taking her in his arms*) Then do. After all, I am your husband. You ought to believe your husband.

PATRICIA I'd like to. But you do keep behaving rather oddly. I thought we were going to have some peace and quiet here.

CHESTER Yes. That's what I thought. And now to add to my troubles your mother's going to set the old man on me. It really is too much! Darling, you do still love me, don't you?

PATRICIA H'm.

CHESTER That's all right, then. (*He kisses her.*)
(*The panel door opens and* MISS PARTRIDGE *puts her head out. They do not see her.*)

MISS P. P'sst!

CHESTER What did you say?

PATRICIA I said 'H'm'. Meaning I still love you.

CHESTER No—after that.

PATRICIA Nothing.

CHESTER Nothing after that?

PATRICIA How could I? You were kissing me.

CHESTER What a good idea!
(*They kiss again.*)

MISS P. P'sst!

CHESTER You said it again.

PATRICIA No, darling.

CHESTER Didn't you hear something? It sort of went——

MISS P. P'sst!

CHESTER Yes—that's it!
(*They turn and see* MISS PARTRIDGE.)
Oh, it's you.

MISS P. So this is where you put it, eh?

CHESTER (*crossing to* C.) Put what?

MISS P. The picture.

CHESTER Picture?

MISS P. The one from up there. The one I saw you and the big Boy Scout taking off the wall. It's in here.

PATRICIA (*furious*) Chester!

CHESTER But that was before!

PATRICIA   And you said you didn't know what had happened to it!
CHESTER   But I can explain——
PATRICIA   Yes, I'm sure you can. You're very good at explaining. But not to me—because I shan't be here!
          (*She storms to the archway and almost collides with* ADA *coming in.*)
PATRICIA   Oooh! (*She goes.*)
          (ADA *moves in, hopefully.* CHESTER *turns on* MISS PARTRIDGE.)
CHESTER   Thank you. Thank you very much.
  MISS P.   Not at all, dear. I thought you'd like to know where it was. (*She closes the panel door and moves* R.) You haven't seen those visitors, have you? I still can't find them.
CHESTER   No. I haven't. (*He turns away to D.L. of the fireplace.*)
  MISS P.   Still, I expect they're having a very interesting time. (*She gazes at the horse in the portrait.*)
CHESTER   (*to* ADA) What do you want?
   ADA   It's that Boy Scout, sir. He's in the downstairs one again.
CHESTER   I don't care if all fifty of them are in the downstairs one!
   ADA   Oh, there wouldn't be room for fifty.
  MISS P.   What a nice kind face.
CHESTER   (*modestly*) Well, I don't know.
  MISS P.   Not you—the horse.
CHESTER   Blast the horse! (*He crosses* ADA *to* D.L.)
   ADA   She was in a bit of a state, sir, wasn't she?
CHESTER   Who—the horse?
   ADA   No—your wife.
CHESTER   Oh, her. Yes, she was.
   ADA   (*to* L. *of the armchair*) Do you think there's any hope?
CHESTER   Hope?
   ADA   That she won't come back?
CHESTER   I should think it's very likely.
   ADA   (*starting to take off her apron*) Then I'd better get ready!
CHESTER   No, Ada—not now!
   ADA   No, sir?
CHESTER   You'd find me very trying. I'm a difficult chap. Always going off in all directions. No—er—what you need, Ada, is a solid, reliable sort of man.

ADA   Oh, yes, sir!

CHESTER   Someone like George.

ADA   George?

CHESTER   The big Boy Scout.

ADA   Oh! The one with my bucket?

CHESTER   The very one! As a matter of fact, he's rather taken a
          fancy to you. Said so to me after you'd gone. Con-
          fidentially, of course—man to man and all that—but
          he said he rather liked you.

ADA   He did?

CHESTER   Yes. Very. He said he liked you very.
          (*She starts to go.*)
          Where are you going?

ADA   To take him back his bucket.

CHESTER   (*to her*) Ada—just a minute. There's something I want
          you to do for me first.

ADA   Oh, yes, sir—anything!

CHESTER   Now, now! Nothing like that. Whoever put that picture
          in there will be back to collect it, so we'd better move
          it first. Will you give me a hand?

ADA   Anything you say, sir.

CHESTER   Right—here we go. (*He goes to the panel door, but can-
          not find it.*) Where's the blasted door? Miss Partridge,
          did you close it? (MISS PARTRIDGE *is on his* R.)

MISS P.   I suppose I must have done. I was engrossed and didn't
          notice.

CHESTER   Well, get unengrossed and help me find it. Do you know
          where it is?
          (*They all search for the door.*)

MISS P.   It was here a moment ago.

ADA   It can't be far, sir.

CHESTER   Blast it! Ada, do you know the other way in—from
          the library?

ADA   Oh, yes, sir.

CHESTER   Good. You come with me. We'll take the picture out
          that way and find somewhere else to hide it. I'd like
          to see old Capone's face when he comes back and finds
          it gone! (*To* MISS PARTRIDGE.) You stay here and be sure
          no one comes in and finds that door. All right?

MISS P. All right!

CHESTER Come on, Ada!

ADA Sir——

CHESTER What is it now? This is urgent.

ADA Do you really think that Boy Scout likes me?

CHESTER I should think if you're at all interested, he'd be a pushover! (*He goes out through the archway.*)

ADA If I'm at all interested? He's a man, isn't he?

(CHESTER *returns.*)

CHESTER Come on! (*He drags her off.*)

(MISS PARTRIDGE *takes a chair and sets it against the wall in the region of the panel door. Then she notices an old assegai on the wall, takes it down and sits near the panel door holding the weapon at the ready.* CAPONE *and* WEDGWOOD *come in from the cellar* D.R. *They move up to the panel door where* MISS PARTRIDGE *faces them with the assegai.*)

MISS P. Go away!

CAPONE What is the trouble?

MISS P. I can't have you here! Go away!

(CAPONE *and* WEDGWOOD *exchange a look. They shrug.* CAPONE *takes* WEDGWOOD's *arm and takes him away to* D.L. *out of earshot of* MISS PARTRIDGE.)

CAPONE We will have to wait for a moment. Now, listen very carefully. (*He glances back at* MISS PARTRIDGE *to make sure she cannot hear him and lowers his voice slightly.*) I will bring the car up to the front door. (WEDGWOOD *nods.*) Now—while the horse is on the wall, the lady is in there behind the door—yes? (WEDGWOOD *nods enthusiastically.*) While I am getting the car and—(*With a nod towards* MISS PARTRIDGE.)—as soon as it is all clear you will remove the lady from behind the door ready to carry out when I return. (WEDGWOOD *nods.*) You had better wrap her up in case we run into anyone. You will find canvas and string in the cellar. You understand? (WEDGWOOD *nods.*) All right. I will be back in five minutes with the car.

(CAPONE *goes off through the archway.* WEDGWOOD *crosses to* D.R. *and goes off into the cellar. As he dis-*

appears MAGGIE *and* BERT *wander in from the study.*)

MAGGIE   Well, don't you remember the way we came in? There must be a way out somewhere.

BERT   It ought to be marked. There ought to be a sign, that's what I say. The amount of money they've taken off me they could afford a sign.

MAGGIE   What's the matter with you? You had a good tea, didn't you? Stuffing your face with all them cream cakes.

BERT   That was hours ago.

MAGGIE   Look, we've got to get out of 'ere. We'll miss the Green Line if we stay much longer.

BERT   (*noticing* MISS PARTRIDGE) 'Ere, look! Over there by the wall. Isn't that that Partridge bird?

MAGGIE   Oh, yes. We'll ask her. She is supposed to be the guide, after all. She'll know the way out.

BERT   You want a bet?

(*They approach* MISS PARTRIDGE *who looks up in alarm, the assegai thrust forward.*)

MISS P.   You can't come in here!

MAGGIE   What?

MISS P.   You can't come in here!

MAGGIE   In where?

MISS P.   Through this door.

MAGGIE   Which door?

MISS P.   I've been given instructions to keep you out.

MAGGIE   Out of where?

MISS P.   Out of there. You can't open this door.

BERT   But there is no door. She's barmy! Come on.

MAGGIE   Miss Partridge, we only want to find the way out.

MISS P.   You won't need the way out.

MAGGIE   Why not?

MISS P.   Because you can't go in.

BERT   We are in, for 'eaven's sake! She's as batty as a coot. Look, we are in!

MISS P.   In?

BERT   In the 'ouse! We paid—remember? And now we want to find the way out. As you're the guide we thought you'd like to do a bit of guiding.

MISS P. I can't leave here! I gave my word. I'm guarding this
door.

MAGGIE You don't have to leave, Miss Partridge. Just tell us
which way.

MISS P. Oh. Oh, yes. Through there. Keep going right. You
can't miss it.

MAGGIE Thank you.

BERT She's round the bend, I tell you. She ought to be kept
in a cage. They could charge another 'alf-a-crown to
look at 'er!

(*They go out through the archway.* LORD ELROOD *comes
down the stairs.*)

ELROOD What the devil are you doing with that?

MISS P. I'm—I'm on guard, Lord Elrood.

ELROOD (*to* R. *of* MISS PARTRIDGE) On guard? Don't tell me
they're calling up the women now. Look here, have
you seen him?

MISS P. Who?

ELROOD You know who. I'm after him, and when I find him he's
going to be a damn sight sorrier than I shall be. Look, I
admire your courage and all that. Very commendable.
But I don't like women in the firing line. You pop in
here until the shooting's over. (*He opens the panel door.*)

MISS P. You know how to open it!

ELROOD In you go.

MISS P. But I—I can't——

ELROOD Too dangerous out here. Lie low there until you get the
all clear. Is that clear?

MISS P Er—yes, Lord Elrood. If you insist.

ELROOD I do insist. Thank God the age of chivalry isn't quite
dead. In you go. (*He bundles her in with the assegai.*)
And no peeping! This is going to be horrible! (*He closes
the panel door on her, and goes out through the
archway.*)

(WEDGWOOD *comes in from the cellar* D.R. *He is carrying a large piece of canvas and a ball of thick string. He
looks about and then goes up to the panel door. He
finds the catch, opens the door and goes in. There is a
loud cry and* WEDGWOOD *reappears at speed, clutching*

his behind in agony. He thinks about his instructions, looks at the canvas and string, decides he must do as he was told, shrugs, opens the panel door and goes in again, closing the door behind him. From within another cry which is stifled abruptly. GEORGE WILLIS *comes in from the archway.*)

GEORGE   I say—I wonder if I could have some——? (*Seeing there is nobody there.*) Oh. (*He moves C., hears a scuffling beyond the panel door, moves up and listens intently.*) (ADA *comes in, carrying a bucket. She goes to him, holds out the bucket, beaming. He turns and sees her.*)

ADA   There you are, sir—you can have it.

GEORGE   (*to her R.*) I beg your pardon?

ADA   The bucket. It's my bucket.

GEORGE   So you said.

ADA   But you can have it.

GEORGE   That's very kind of you. (*He takes it, notices her gazing at him adoringly.*) Thank you. (*He backs away to L. of the sofa.*)

ADA   (*following him*) Is there anything else of mine you'd like?

GEORGE   Not just now, thank you.

ADA   You only have to ask.

GEORGE   I'll remember. I say, just now when I came in I heard scuffling behind the woodwork.

ADA   It'll be the mice, sir.

GEORGE   Pretty big mice.

ADA   They've been there a long time. (*Moving in nearer.*) I heard about you, sir.

GEORGE   Did you? Good heavens! What about me?

ADA   About your feelings.
(*More noises are heard from inside. He escapes below the sofa to R. of it.*)

GEORGE   There! There it was again! Did you hear it?

ADA   (*pursuing him*) It's all right by me, sir!

GEORGE   What are you talking about? (*To above the sofa.*)

ADA   You needn't be embarrassed. You can tell me to my face. I won't spurn you.

GEORGE   Won't you?

ADA   I've never spurned anyone in my life! And I can tell you
now that your feelings for me are entirely reciprocitated.

GEORGE   Reciprocitated? Good heavens! What feelings are you
talking about?

ADA   Your love, sir—your love for me!

GEORGE   What? Now, look here—there must be some mistake——

ADA   Come on, George—take me! I'm ready!

GEORGE   Ready?

ADA   My case is in the hall. I've packed.

GEORGE   Then you'll have to unpack. (*Making for the archway.*)
I've got fifty boys out there waiting for dinner, and
I've got to be off——

ADA   (*following*) There's always after dinner.

GEORGE   If you'll excuse me—I really must go——

ADA   I'll come with you. I've got you now and you're not
getting away from me! (*She pursues him off.*)
(*The panel door opens and* WEDGWOOD *peers out, sees
all is clear and goes back inside. He re-appears bringing*
MISS PARTRIDGE *with him. She is gagged with a handkerchief and is wrapped in canvas from neck to knees
and tied with string like a parcel. He brings her down*
C. CAPONE *comes in from the archway.*)

CAPONE   Are you ready? (*Sees* MISS PARTRIDGE.) What's this?
(WEDGWOOD *shrugs and points to the panel door.*)
You fool! I told you to wrap up the lady in the *portrait*!
(WEDGWOOD *points to panel door.* CAPONE *looks inside.*)
It's gone! Where is it?
(WEDGWOOD *shrugs.*)
Mr. Dreadnought will pay for this!
(*A loud report off-stage.*)
Quick!
(*They push* MISS PARTRIDGE *and she sits on the sofa.
They go out through the panel door and close it behind
them.* CHESTER *runs in from the archway. He is carry-
ing his jacket. He moves to C., sees* MISS PARTRIDGE *and
reacts.*)

CHESTER   Good heavens—Miss Partridge! I didn't know you were
leaving.

(MISS PARTRIDGE *makes unintelligible noises.* CHESTER
removes the gag from her mouth.)
What on earth have you been doing to yourself?

MISS P. Nothing!

CHESTER Well, something terrible's happened.

MISS P. I was assaulted!

CHESTER Congratulations!

MISS P. By a man!

CHESTER What sort of man?

MISS P. A man in a suit.

CHESTER Assaulted by a man in a suit? Incredible!

MISS P. Get me out! Get me out!

CHESTER Yes—of course.

(*He is about to untie her when voices are heard off. For
a moment he is undecided what to do, then he replaces
the gag in* MISS PARTRIDGE'*s mouth and puts his jacket
over her head and sits beside her.* MAGGIE *and* BERT
wander in from the study to C.)

BERT I told you she was barmy. There's no way out there.

MAGGIE I expect we took the wrong turning.

(*They stop as they see* CHESTER *and the anonymous
shape beside him on the sofa.* CHESTER *smiles cheerfully,
waves to them.*)

CHESTER Good afternoon!

BERT Well, if it isn't Charles the Second again.

(*They look inquiringly at the shape beside* CHESTER *as a
noise is heard from beneath the jacket.*)

CHESTER Oh—er—my aunt. She's very shy.

(MAGGIE *and* BERT *exchange a look.*)

BERT Oh. I see.

ELROOD (*off*) Marcellus! Stand by to attack! The blighter's in
there!

(CHESTER *leaps up in panic.*)

CHESTER (*indicating the shape on the sofa*) Here, I say, look after
this for me, will you? (*He races off upstairs.*)

(MAGGIE *and* BERT, *puzzled, sit either side of* MISS PART-
RIDGE. LORD ELROOD *pounds in from the archway to C.*)

ELROOD Which way?

BERT Eh?

ELROOD Which way! Which way!

BERT Which way what?

ELROOD Did he go?

MAGGIE ⎫
BERT   ⎭ (together) That way. (She indicates R., he L.)

ELROOD What have you got under there?

MAGGIE Er—I——

ELROOD Let's have a look! (He lifts the jacket and looks under-
neath, replaces it quickly.) Oh, my God! (He races off
up the stairs.)

MAGGIE You certainly get your money's worth here, don't you?
I mean, there's more going on here than at the Duke of
Bedford's place.
(GEORGE comes in from the archway at the double. He
hesitates C. for a moment.)

GEORGE Good afternoon!
(He crosses D.L., opens the chest and steps inside. They
are watching him.)

GEORGE I shan't be long. (He lies down inside and closes the lid.)

BERT Here—'ave you got the sandwiches?

MAGGIE Yes.

BERT Well, come on, then. May as well 'ave one while we're
waiting.

MAGGIE All right. I am a bit peckish. (Starts to get out sandwiches, looks at MISS PARTRIDGE.) What about——?

BERT Auntie? Well, she can't eat with that on, can she?

MAGGIE Do you think we ought to take it off?

BERT Now, Maggie, he didn't say nothing about taking it
off, did he?

MAGGIE No, but——

BERT Then she stays as she is. Give us a sandwich.
(ADA races in from the archway. She stops as she sees
them.)

ADA Excuse me. (She runs off D.R.)

MAGGIE Egg or cucumber?
(CHESTER races on from the cellar D.R., crosses to D.L.
and opens the chest.)

CHESTER Oh—occupied. (He closes the lid again and runs off,
through the study door U.L.)

BERT Cucumber, I think. I always say it's refreshing is
· cucumber.

(LADY ELROOD *comes down the stairs to above the* R. *end
of the sofa, sees* MAGGIE *and* BERT *sitting either side of
the shape in the middle.*)

LADY E. What on earth——? Is that yours?

MAGGIE No. We're just minding it for a friend.

(LADY ELROOD *whips the jacket off* MISS PARTRIDGE's
head and reacts at what she sees.)

LADY E. Miss Partridge, what are you doing in there? (*Takes the
gag from her mouth.*) This is no time for games!

MISS P. That man did it.

LADY E. (*turning on* BERT) How dare you?

MISS P. No, not him—the one in the bright suit who never talks.
He found me and tied me up.

LADY E. Found you?

MISS P. In the wall.

LADY E. (*moving down on* R. *of the sofa*) What were you doing
in the wall, Miss Partridge?

MISS P. Waiting for the all clear. (*Turning to* MAGGIE.) But I
never heard it. Then they sat me on the sofa and left
me. Then that young man came in and covered me over
with his jacket.

LADY E. Unforgivable!

MAGGIE Would you like a sandwich?

LADY E. No, thank you.

MAGGIE Cucumber.

LADY E. Oh, well in that case. (*Takes one.*) Thank you very much.
(*Starts to eat, crossing below the sofa to* D.C.) I promise
you, Miss Partridge—(*Breaks off and turns to* MAGGIE.)—
h'm—very nice. Very nice indeed.

BERT I always say it's refreshing is cucumber.

MISS P. (*plaintively*) Can I get out of this now?

(*The lid of the chest opens and* GEORGE *arises like
Lazarus.* LADY ELROOD *watches in amazement. He sees
them.*)

GEORGE I'm so sorry. (*He descends again and closes the lid.*)

(LADY ELROOD *goes to the chest. She knocks on the lid.*
GEORGE *opens it a little and peers out.*)

LADY E. (*gently*) Hide and seek, Mr. Willis?

GEORGE (*laughing self-consciously*) Yes—rather!

LADY E. (*loudly*) The game is over!

GEORGE (*climbing out, lamely*) I just thought I'd have a little lie down.

MISS P. Will somebody please come and untie me?

LADY E. Mr. Willis—you're a Boy Scout—you should be good at knots.

GEORGE Yes, of course. (*He goes towards* MISS PARTRIDGE.)

(ADA *races in from* R. MAGGIE *is now pouring tea from a thermos for* BERT *and herself.*)

ADA George!

(*He sees her and bolts for the archway. She pursues him at the double. They race off.*)

LADY E. I think everybody's gone mad. (*To L. of the sofa.*) Now, Miss Partridge, after those two men pushed you onto the sofa where did they go?

MISS P. Through that door in the wall.

LADY E. Right! (*Moving to the panel door.*) You stay there.

MISS P. Won't you untie me first?

LADY E. (*opening the panel door slightly*) Got it first time! (*She flings it open wide and peers inside.*) Anybody there? (*No answer.*) Better make sure. (*She goes out through the panel door.*)

MISS P. Don't leave me here!

(GEORGE *races in from the study door.*)

GEORGE Have you seen her?

MISS P. (*miserably*) She's gone in there!

GEORGE Good!

(*He closes the panel door with a bang and leans against it. From within we hear* LADY ELROOD *knocking on the door.*)

(*Smiling.*) That'll soon cool you off!

(CHESTER *comes in from the archway, carrying something wrapped in paper.*)

CHESTER George! Just the man I need to help me.

GEORGE (*holding the door against the pressure from within*) Well, I'm rather tied up at the moment.

MISS P. (*angrily*) So am I!

CHESTER I say—what have you got in there?

GEORGE The—the maid. I'm trying to escape. Would you mind holding this for a moment?

CHESTER Doesn't sound like the maid to me.

MISS P. It's not the maid!

GEORGE But I asked you and you said——

MISS P. It's Lady Elrood!

GEORGE Oh, my God!

BERT 'Ere—'ave you got another cucumber sandwich?

(CHESTER *puts down his parcel* L. *of the fireplace and moves to* GEORGE.)

GEORGE Shall I let her out?

CHESTER Can you think of an alternative?

GEORGE We could run.

CHESTER Not fast enough.

(GEORGE *opens the panel door and* LADY ELROOD *bursts out, bearing the assegai and looking ready to use it.* CHESTER *and* GEORGE *back away towards the armchair. She follows.*)

LADY E. Who—did—that?

GEORGE Er—it was—it was me—I——

LADY E. You, Mr. Willis?

GEORGE A mistake. It was a mistake.

LADY E. It was your last mistake. (*She advances on him with the assegai.*)

CHESTER (*getting between them*) Ah!—er—Lady—er—Mother—yes—it was a mistake——

LADY E. I'll deal with you later. Get out of my way.

CHESTER You see he thought you were the maid.

LADY E. Oh, did he?

GEORGE (*quickly*) I don't mean you looked like the maid.

LADY E. No?

GEORGE Oh, no—you're nothing like her. (*To* CHESTER.) Is she?

CHESTER Not the slightest.

LADY E. Then why did he think I was her?

CHESTER Yes—a good question. (*To* GEORGE.) Have you got one for that?

GEORGE I'll have to go.

CHESTER Good idea. We'll both go.

(*They start to move below the armchair to* L.C.)

LADY E. Just a minute!

CHESTER Ah! Too late to go.

LADY E. I'm not letting either of you out of my sight again.

CHESTER Not ever?

LADY E. Not until I get to the bottom of it.

CHESTER (*looking at the assegai*) Yes. I see what you mean.

(PATRICIA *runs in from the archway, distraught. She comes to* C., *on the* R. *of* LADY ELROOD.)

PATRICIA Mummy! Mummy!

CHESTER Are you still here?

PATRICIA Mummy—they've got it!

LADY E. What are you talking about?

PATRICIA Those two men—Mr. Capone and Mr. Wedgwood—they've got it!

CHESTER And as far as I'm concerned they can keep it! (*To* GEORGE.) What's she talking about?

GEORGE Haven't the foggiest.

CHESTER That makes two.

(*They shake hands.*)

LADY E. Now, calm down, darling—what is it that they've got?

PATRICIA The picture—your picture from up there!

LADY E. The lady?

PATRICIA Yes! I saw them coming out of the library carrying it between them. I shouted to them but they ran off.

LADY E. We'll have to stop them.

CHESTER You didn't believe me, did you? I tried to warn you.

LADY E. This is no time for recrimination!

CHESTER I should jolly well think not.

PATRICIA Chester, how can you stand there? Do something!

CHESTER There's nothing to be done.

PATRICIA You mean you're going to let them get away with £20,000?

LADY E. £20,000?

PATRICIA Ask Mr. Willis. He's an expert.

GEORGE I may be wrong, Lady Elrood, but it's possible.

LADY E. £20,000? How many two-and-sixes is that?

PATRICIA Chester, we've got to get it back!

CHESTER We already have.

PATRICIA What?

LADY E. What did you say?

CHESTER It's here!

PATRICIA Here?

CHESTER Ada and I moved it for safe-keeping. We put it in the downstairs one. I don't know what old Capone's going off with but your portrait's here.

PATRICIA Let's see it.

CHESTER Still doubting my word, eh?
(*He brings down the package to between* PATRICIA *and* LADY ELROOD *and takes off the cover with a flourish. It is a portrait. They gasp. It is a portrait of a white horse.*)

LADY E. It's a horse!

CHESTER What? (*He looks.*) They've done it again! (*He sees* LADY ELROOD *advancing with the assegai.*) Now, now—no—no, please!—I can explain——
(*He races out through the archway, pursued by* LADY ELROOD *with the assegai and followed by* PATRICIA.)

MISS P. (*rising with difficulty*) Will somebody please untie me!
(GEORGE *goes to her, but* ADA *comes in from the study and he runs out D.R. with her in hot pursuit.* MISS PARTRIDGE *is now standing C., still wrapped in canvas and tied up from neck to knees.*)

BERT Any more tea in there, luv?

MAGGIE Just a drop. (*She pours tea.*)

BERT Ta.
(LORD ELROOD *pounds on down the stairs with his shotgun at the ready.*)

ELROOD They're attacking! Action stations! Pick your target and fire! (*Reaches* MISS PARTRIDGE.) Now, now—you're in the firing line again. Come along!

MISS P. But, Lord Elrood, I——

ELROOD In you go! (*He pushes her out through the panel door and closes it. He then runs off through the archway.*)
(CHESTER *runs in from the study door pursued by* LADY ELROOD *and* PATRICIA. *They cross in front of* MAGGIE *and* BERT *and go off into the cellar D.R.*
MISS PARTRIDGE *staggers out of the panel door and makes her way as best she can to C.*

GEORGE *runs down the stairs pursued by* ADA. *They cross below the sofa, in turn catch hold of* MISS PARTRIDGE *and spin her round, and race off up the stairs again.*

PATRICIA *and* LADY ELROOD *run out of the cellar pursued by* CHESTER *carrying the assegai. They also spin the unfortunate* MISS PARTRIDGE *round as they pass and run off through the study door.*

GEORGE, *pursued by* LORD ELROOD *and followed by* ADA, *races down the stairs and out into the study.* MISS PARTRIDGE, *spinning wildly, staggers out through the panel door again.*

Throughout this MAGGIE *and* BERT, *sipping tea and eating sandwiches, watch the events happily.*

LADY ELROOD, *breathless, supported by* PATRICIA, *comes in from the archway to C.)*

LADY E.   I can't go on any longer. I'm quite exhausted!

BERT   Come and sit over here, luv.

(LADY ELROOD *sits L. of* BERT. PATRICIA *is* C.)

MAGGIE   'Ere you are—'ave a cup of tea, dear.

LADY E.   Thank you so much. (*She takes it gratefully.*)

MAGGIE   You are an energetic family, aren't you?

LADY E.   (*to* PATRICIA) Do you think they'll get away with it?

PATRICIA   Don't worry—Chester went after them.

LADY E.   It's that that makes me worry.

(CHESTER *comes in from the archway carrying the portrait (out of the frame) aloft. He comes to L. of* PATRICIA.)

CHESTER   Got it! (*With sudden fear.*) I say, it is the real one this time, isn't it?

PATRICIA   Yes, darling, that's the real one all right.

CHESTER   I didn't wait to look. I just grabbed it from old Capone and ran like the clappers.

PATRICIA   Do you think they'll get away?

CHESTER   Have you ever tried to fight your way through fifty Boy Scouts? They'll be lucky to get out alive.

PATRICIA   Oh, darling! (*She kisses him.*)

(LADY ELROOD *rises and gently takes the portrait from* CHESTER's *hands. He emerges from the embrace.*)

CHESTER   H'm?

LADY E. I think *I'd* better take care of this, don't you?

CHESTER Oh, yes—rather!

LADY E. (*going R.*) £20,000! The grocer will be pleased! (*She goes off upstairs.*)

(GEORGE *runs in from the study pursued by* ADA, *who now carries the assegai.*)

GEORGE Now, now! Ada! It's very dangerous! Put it down! (*He backs away from her to below the armchair.*)

ADA Not unless you surrender, sir.

GEORGE (*turning to* CHESTER) What shall I do?

CHESTER I thought you Boy Scouts were supposed to be prepared.

GEORGE Not for this.

CHESTER I should surrender then.

(GEORGE *looks helplessly at* ADA. *She puts down the assegai and moves to him.*)

PATRICIA Darling—can you ever forgive me?

CHESTER Forgive you?

PATRICIA For doubting you.

CHESTER I might. If you play your cards well.

PATRICIA How?

(CHESTER *turns and looks at* GEORGE. *They both shrug and turn simultaneously to kiss the girls.*

MAGGIE *and* BERT *are busy eating.*

CAPONE *and* WEDGWOOD *run in through the archway to C. They are dressed as Boy Scouts.* LORD ELROOD *appears from the cellar D.R. and gives a shout as he sees them. They race back towards the archway with* ELROOD *in hot pursuit. The two couples are kissing.* MAGGIE *and* BERT *shrug and follow suit.*)

CURTAIN

PRODUCTION NOTE

Post Horn Gallop was written primarily as a sequel to my earlier farce, *Wild Goose Chase*, and most of the characters in the first play re-appear in this one. I hope you will enjoy meeting and playing them again. But *Post Horn Gallop* is, nevertheless, an entirely separate entity and production need not depend on whether you have previously presented *Wild Goose Chase*.

There is always a temptation when acting and directing farce to go too far. It is amazing how many professional actors and actresses wrongly assume that if a play bears the label of 'farce' it is a licence to dress up like a dog's dinner and behave in a completely unreal manner. It is the *situations* in farce which are larger than life, and the more *real* the characters are in these situations then the funnier the result.

Another myth that should be exploded very early in production is that farce has to be raced along at a breathless pace, leaving the audience not only exhausted but having also missed half the points of the play. Ralph Lynn would never have been caught racing through a scene without time for thought. Even the most lunatic line will have greater effect if it is said as a result of thought and not gabbled out like a ticker-tape machine. For instance, the scene about the horse (Act III, page 70) will be funnier if Chester's explanations are well thought out and put forward as sensible suggestions and not as a series of 'gags'. Naturally, this does not apply to all scenes in the play, and the good director will vary the pace of different scenes according to their context.

Chester Dreadnought is obviously the linchpin of the production, but the success of the play depends on the team work of the whole cast. Chester cannot carry the play alone. The actor who plays him must genuinely believe in the situations and react in a truthful manner. But he must also discipline those reactions. If he plays the whole thing in a never-ending state of visual jitters we shall soon tire of him.

It is important that he must have an inherent sense of fun, so that even in the most desperate situation with Capone and Wedgwood there is always a tiny part of him which stands outside and really rather enjoys it all. It is this quality that singles out the real farceur from the rest.

Lord Elrood lives in an imaginary world of his own, and he must never step out of this world. It is his complete and utter belief that the postman is a spy and that Marcellus and Horatio exist that makes him a funny character. He should be dressed as a country gentleman and played with verve. Lady Elrood is long-suffering, well-dressed and delightfully vague, while Patricia is attractive and vivacious.

Miss Partridge is intense, voluble and eccentric. This is a very rewarding part for a character actress, but again—complete sincerity is the keynote. Remember, people like Miss Partridge do exist. We have all met her at one time or another. Moving about the stage with business-like authority, listening intently and suddenly to echoes of mediaeval times, searching with loving care for historic relics, she can keep the audience chuckling continuously.

Ada, the maid, is stupid, but should *not* behave as if she had recently escaped from an asylum. She is rather in awe of Lord Elrood, impatient with Lady Elrood and in love with Chester. She is unhappy at the beginning when her love is not reciprocated, but finds consolation in the shape of George Willis. The more we believe in her, the more we shall laugh.

Bert and Maggie are a middle-aged Cockney couple on a sightseeing trip, and at Elrood Castle that day there is plenty to see. It is through their eyes that we enjoy many of the lunatic situations in the play, and the tea scene in Act II can be a riot. The 'business' I have listed in the book for this scene need not be the final word—I hope that many actors and directors will dream up suitable alternatives of their own—but it has been tried and works well. Bert and Maggie must be played slowly to maintain the correct balance.

George Willis is about 40, solid, dependable—and vulnerable. He should be played with enthusiasm. Size is, of course, immaterial but I did visualize him as being a large man. To me there is something funnier about a large scoutmaster—especially in his vulnerability!

Finally, the two crooks, Mr. Capone and Mr. Wedgwood. It is important that their threat should be private between themselves and Chester. To the rest of the cast—especially Lady Elrood and

Patricia—they must appear as ordinary acceptable visitors to the castle. Dress them up like something out of *West Side Story* and we shall never be able to believe that Lady Elrood could be taken in by them.

Good luck with your production!

D.B.

PROPERTY PLOT

ACT ONE

SET:

Box of groceries (off L. ADA)
Shotgun (off R. ELROOD)
Cup of coffee (off L. LADY ELROOD)
Newspaper (Armchair table. PATRICIA)
Handbag (off L. MISS PARTRIDGE)
Mallet (off L. MISS PARTRIDGE)
Magnifying glass (off L. MISS PARTRIDGE)
'Guide' armband (Mantelpiece. LADY ELROOD)
Suitcase (off L. CHESTER)
Bandages (off L. PATRICIA)
Large handbag (off L. MAGGIE)
Ticket machine (off L. MISS PARTRIDGE)

PERSONAL:

Cigarette-case with cigarettes (CHESTER)
Four half-crowns (BERT)
£1 note (BERT)

ACT TWO

SET:

Small suitcase (off L. ADA)
Rose in vase (Mantelpiece. ADA)
Tea trolley (off L. ADA)
    On it:
        Tea pot
        Milk jug
        Sugar basin (lumps)
        4 cups
        4 saucers
        Dish of muffins

Plate of cakes
Biscuits
Tea spoons
Cake forks
Bucket (off L. GEORGE)

PERSONAL :
Watch (LADY ELROOD)
Letter (GEORGE)

ACT THREE

SET :
Bucket (off L. GEORGE)
Portrait of brown horse's head (off R. CAPONE)
Assegai (on wall U.R. MISS PARTRIDGE)
Large piece of canvas (off R. WEDGWOOD)
Ball of thick string (off R. WEDGWOOD)
Packet of sandwiches (in MAGGIE's bag)
Thermos (MAGGIE's bag)
2 cups (MAGGIE's bag)
Portrait of white horse's head wrapped in brown paper (off L.
CHESTER)

PERSONAL :
Handkerchief (WEDGWOOD)

EFFECTS

Telephone bell
7 gun shots (Act I)
2 gun shots (Act II)
2 gun shots (Act III)
Echo response from chimney (Act I)
Creaking door (Acts II and III)

MUSIC

'Post Horn Gallop' before the curtain rises on each Act.

COSTUME PLOT

CHESTER
  Casual suit, raincoat.

LORD ELROOD
  Brown tweed jacket, corduroy trousers, waistcoat and cravat.

LADY ELROOD
  Housecoat (Act I).
  Wool dress (Act I).
  Change of dress (Act II).
  Evening blouse and skirt (Act III).

PATRICIA
  Dress, coat and hat (Acts I and II).
  Change of dress (Act III).

MISS PARTRIDGE
  Tweed costume, flat shoes, felt hat, beads.

GEORGE
  Scout uniform.

ADA
  Maid's uniform, raincoat and hat.

MAGGIE
  Skirt and blouse, flat shoes, coat and hat.

BERT
  Sports coat and flannels, cap.

MR. CAPONE
  Dark blue suit, raincoat, trilby hat.
  Scout uniform (Act III).

MR. WEDGWOOD
  Loud check suit, hat.
  Scout uniform (Act III).

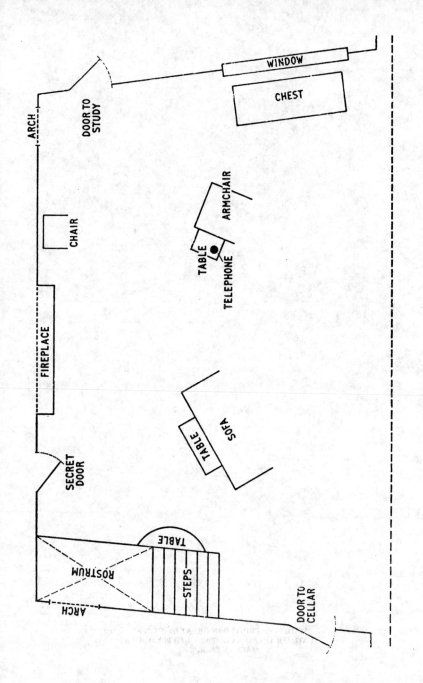

MADE AND PRINTED IN GREAT BRITAIN BY
LATIMER TREND & COMPANY LTD PLYMOUTH
MADE IN ENGLAND